S0-ATM-188

America's New Breed Of Entrepreneurs

Learn how America's successful entrepreneurs use these SIX MAXIMS OF ENTREPRENEURIAL MARKETING to remain leaders in their marketplaces:

One: *The Problem-Solving Approach*

Innovate the obvious; cultivate quality; create the product that solves a problem.

Two: *The Entrepreneurial Difference*

I am what you are . . . but, I'm better! In a sea of similarity, make your product stand out: Let them eat *your* cake.

Three: *The Target Practice Proverb*

Aim for *your* market and shoot to sell; pinpoint your market and never let it go.

Four: *The Presentation Principle*

Capture the market with captivating concepts; use the *right* method for your message.

Five: *The Open-Throttle Theory*

Use all your tools and talents; hit the market with everything you've got.

Six: *The Selling Code*

Sell hard; sell often.

America's New Breed Of Entrepreneurs

Their Marketing Strategies, Techniques, and Successes

Jeffrey L. Seglin

ACROPOLIS BOOKS LTD.
WASHINGTON, D.C.

To Nancy

Now in her beauty's wake my song can thrust
Its following flight no farther; I give o'er
As, at his art's end, every artist must.

Dante's *Paradiso*, Canto XXX, 31-3

 Portions of chapters 8, 13, and 22 originally appeared in *Inc.* magazine under the titles "The Direct Approach" (September 1984), "Putting On a Good Face" (November 1984), and "Screen Test" (July 1984). The information has been updated and expanded for use in this book. Reprinted with permission, *Inc.* Magazine. Copyright ©1984. Inc. Publishing Corporation, 38 Commercial Wharf, Boston, MA 02110.

ACROPOLIS BOOKS, LTD.
Colortone Building, 2400 17th St., N.W.,
Washington, D.C. 20009

Printed in the United States of America by
COLORTONE PRESS
Creative Graphics, Inc.
Washington, D.C. 20009

Library of Congress Cataloging-in-Publication Data

Seglin, Jeffrey L., 1956-
America's new breed of entrepreneurs.

Includes index.
1. Marketing—United States. 2. Entrepreneur.
I. Title.
HF5415.1.S44 1985 658.8 85-26766
ISBN 0-87491-788-3

Acknowledgments

Traveling around the country looking for an interesting marketing story is no easy task. I owe many friends and people thanks for their help in completing the research and interviews that went into this book.

First, I must thank all the people and businesses mentioned throughout the text. Dozens of people tolerated my intrusions into their hectic schedules and allowed me to pry into their personal business affairs.

Others I must thank who put me in touch with business owners or gave me the benefit of their ideas are: Alison Krawiec, John Waggoner, Melanie Ripley (managing editor of Madison, Wisconsin's *In Business Magazine)*, Bob Pettegrew, Kimmel King, Tim Smith, David McDonnell, Marilyn Heise, Bob Roen, Jeanne and Billy Berrigan, Nancy Moss, and Joan Kenney.

Many also shared their hospitality while I was on the road. To the people of Ed's and Eats-U-Want who gave me countless coffee refills, the Silvermans who took me to Grand Forks' finest, Flo Lewis who fed me what has to be the finest eggplant parmigiana on the east coast, and Sid Beshkin I owe thanks. To Howard, Patti, David, and Brian Palay; Yvonne Surette; Martha Jewett; Ralph Hamilton; Joanne Thomson; Cae Long; Jim and Claire Henderson; and to my parents, Lester and Beverly Seglin, I owe thanks for sharing their homes and lending encouragement.

I also owe my agent, Evan Marshall, my thanks not only for his encouragement and suggestions while I was writing, but also for his patience and for marketing my book proposal in the first place.

The people at *Acropolis Books* have been enthusiastic from the start when Laurie Tag and Kathleen Hughes first called me to share their excitement about the project. Dan Wallace, who took over the project and has believed steadfastly in it throughout his involvement, has been a good sounding board for many of my ideas. Phil Trupp's editing and Al Hackl's commitment to the project have strengthened the book's focus.

Eddie, Bethany, and their mother, Nancy, lived with me throughout the months of travel, phone interviews, and long nights of writing. Their tolerance, love, and support has been a blessing.

While ultimately I am responsible for the information in this book, I must acknowledge Jim Lewis and Nancy Long Coleman, who read the manuscript line by line. Many of their suggestions have helped shaped the book. They are not only my close friends, but also two of the finest professional editors I know.

Contents

MAXIM TWO: THE ENTREPRENEURIAL DIFFERENCE

MAXIM THREE: THE TARGET-PRACTICE PROVERB

MAXIM SIX: THE SELLING CODE

Introduction

The entrepreneurial spirit has captured the fascination of mainstream America. It's no longer only the small businessperson or business owner alone who shares the fascination. There is clearly a growing interest in how businesses work, why they work, and how "ordinary" people can share in or add their own unique perspective to the business world.

With estimates that more than a half million businesses are started every year, there's a strong likelihood that every time you turn the corner you run the risk of bumping into an entrepreneurial soul. With politicians dubbing this the "age of the entrepreneur," it's become fashionable to struggle it out on your own venture.

America's New Breed of Entrepreneurs is a new addition to a growing list of business books, but its approach is unique. It asks—and answers—the key questions: How do entrepreneurs think? How do they develop their products? What are they actually doing in the marketplace? And, most importantly, how do they make the whole marketing process work?

This book can be used as a training tool for marketing professionals and sales forces. Professionals can learn from the profiles which are presented here. They can learn about the innovations, new technologies, and ingenuity being used by people who are out there doing what they do well. The focus of this book is on marketing because marketing is so obviously crucial to the success of any entrepreneur. If there is no market, there is no success. If there are no sales, there is no business. If there is no awareness of the product, no matter how limited that awareness needs to be, there is little chance of survival. Marketing is a broad discipline and it lies at the core of many entrepreneurial success stories.

The businesses profiled here are small to mid-size businesses. Part of the reason for this is that there is a great deal of innovation and experimentation with marketing going on at this level. Another reason is that the perception that people start a business with the express purpose of growing a giant corporation that can be sold off to the highest bidder is not particularly well-founded. There are those who see their businesses as an investment in a lifestyle.

In fact, if the results of a study conducted by Dr. Paul D. Reynolds, a sociology professor at the University of Minnesota, are correct, it seems that the majority of businesses these days are not started to grow large. In his "1984 Minnesota New Firm Study," Reynolds (along with Research Associate Steven West and the sponsorship of the University of Minnesota Center for Urban and Regional Affairs) studied 551 new Minnesota firms which started in the six years prior to 1984.

"The study confirms that 90 percent of new businesses start at home," Reynolds told me. "I don't mean in their garage, but in their community, where the entrepreneur feels comfortable and has a personal safety net if things go wrong."

The average firm in the Minnesota study (categories included agriculture, construction, manufacturing, distributive services, producer services, retail, and consumer services) began with $71,000 of prestart financing. Of this average, $33,000 came from personal savings, $9,000 from foregone salaries, $6,000 from relatives and kin, $2,000 from kin, $3,000 from suppliers extending credit, and the remaining $18,000 from other sources.

The study also found that the majority of firms started are "lifestyle" firms, which are designed to stay small with very gradual growth. "What we found, much to our surprise," says Reynolds, "is that roughly two-thirds of the firms were started by people who appear to want a comfortable life—stay small, grow sales very gradually."

"Low start-up/low growth" firms (firms with first year sales of less than $250,000 and an average growth rate of less than $100,000 a year) were 61 percent of all new firms. "High start-up/high growth" firms (those with first year sales of more than $250,000 and growth rates in excess of $100,000 a year) were only 16 percent of new firms.

An important result of findings like those of the Minnesota Study is that the "little guy," the new entrepreneur, can now be assured that he or she is not alone out there, battling marketing windmills in the dark. Others are battling it out, too. In many cases they are winning more battles than they are losing, since some of the firms in the Minnesota study have already been around for six years.

Reports estimating the failure rate of new businesses seem to put a damper on some entrepreneurial optimism. With reports ranging as high as 85 percent of new ventures failing, who would want to risk it? It's reminiscent of sitting in a freshman orientation meeting in college, listening to the Dean announce, "Look to your left, look to your right—one, and in some cases two, of those students sitting next to you will not make it through to graduation."

Some experts, such as David Birch, MIT professor and the founder of Cognetics, Inc., argue that the death rate of small businesses is greatly exaggerated, that the failures over the first decade or so come closer to 50 percent. What's more, the "failures" in this 50 percent group don't go bankrupt as often as they decide to shift business ventures or go to work for someone else.

The going's rough, but the practical marketing savvy and persistence of today's entrepreneurs makes success possible. The new entrepreneurs learn the marketing ropes of their respective trades, apply seat-of-the-pants logic and innovative maneuvers, bring their product or service to market—and make it work.

Profiles of companies located throughout the country are used in this book not only because it introduces dozens of captivating personalities, but also because it captures the spirit of entrepreneurial marketing without bombarding the reader with obtuse technical language that disguises what lies at the heart of the issues. By focusing on the players in the field who are changing the face of how concepts and products are marketed and sold, the reader can get caught up in the process.

You can struggle with Steve Silverman, who is caught in a static marketplace with no apparent opportunities for growth, as he daringly experiments with the unproven videotex technology to see if he can bring his North Dakota clothier expertise to a potentially limitless market. You can exude confidence with David Gilvar and David Burr who know that with the proper corporate identity and marketing savvy, they can take the company they started with a cardboard prototype and no capital and build it into a multi-million dollar company that controls more than 75 percent of its market. You can experiment with Stephen Garber who wants to expand his wine business from a storefront operation to a distributor of fine wines to sophisticated clients. Or you can hope with Niles Barto that the new technology of low power television can give him and his auto repair business an affordable and effective marketing avenue in LaSalle, Illinois.

Throughout the stories of marketing, not only is the marketer's story told, but in the process the marketing concepts, technology, and applicability to a reader's interest or situation unfolds.

Anyone who in any way has ever been intrigued by the possibility of starting his or her own business should find these stories useful. Anyone interested in how others have successfully used marketing ingenuity will find this book to be a good read. Anyone fascinated with the way various cross-sections of America view the rest of the country will find this book revealing. Anyone interested in popular culture might find the stories in this book amusing, enlightening, and enriching. Anyone who is fascinated with the process of developing effective solutions to problems—sometimes methodologically, sometimes through serendipity—just might find this book enthralling.

Jeffrey L. Seglin

Boston, Massachusetts
1985

Learn how America's new breed of entrepreneurs uses these SIX MAXIMS OF ENTREPRENEURIAL MARKETING to remain leaders in the marketplace:

One	*The Problem-Solving Approach:* Innovate the obvious. Cultivate quality. Create the product that solves a problem.
Two	*The Entrepreneurial Difference:* I am what you are . . . but I'm better. In a sea of similarity, make your product stand out. Let them eat your cake.
Three	*The Target-Practice Proverb:* Aim for *your* market and shoot to sell. Pinpoint your market and never let it go.
Four	*The Presentation Principle:* Capture your market with captivating concepts. Use the *right* method for your message.
Five	*The Open-Throttle Theory:* Use all your tools and talents. Hit the market with everything you've got.
Six	*The Selling Code:* Sell hard. Sell often.

Maxim One

The Problem-Solving Approach

Innovate the Obvious.
Cultivate Quality.
Create the Product
that Solves a Problem.

Starting from scratch is tough. It's easy enough to tell yourself you want to start a business. But when the time comes to decide what your product or service is going to be, how easy is it then?

At the heart of the marketing process is the product. If you want to market something, you've obviously got to have something to market.

This first part of *America's New Breed of Entrepreneurs* explores how products or services have been given birth. What's gone into product development? How crucial a role has market research played in product development? Has quality control had an impact on marketing?

In the course of talking with businesspeople around the country, it became clear to me that, while there may be similarities in execution, no two companies come up with products in exactly the same way. Some strive to make sure that the ultimate product reflects both their personal lifestyles and beliefs. Others hope that their product or service might fill a void they recognize in the marketplace. Still others approach product development with more of a "gee whiz, that'd be a great product" approach. The variations and combinations of product development techniques vary widely, as you'll see from the businesses profiled here.

You'll also note that these companies are committed to market research and product quality. The companies gather, record, and analyze market data and apply it throughout the development of their products and services. And they're also quick to recognize that, although it might mean higher production costs in the short run, strong quality control standards will garner an even higher market share in the long run, particularly in turbulent economic times when the potential marketplace may be looking to get the most bang for the buck.

The gestation period for the birth of a product will, of course, vary from company to company. In the process of this marketing journey, however, perhaps you'll come away with the notion that these people have succeeded because they believe in what they're doing. They may fail from time to time, or develop a product which hits the market with a resounding thud, but they don't allow minor setbacks to sway them. These entrepreneurs believe in what they're doing and that ultimately the marketplace will share their belief.

Chapter One

Product Development: Disciplined Exuberance

PHILOSOPHICAL FOOD

In 1962, in a small grocery store-luncheonette in Worcester, Massachusetts, called "George's," a product was born. For about 20 years, Hannah and George Kalajian had been running George's with moderate success. George ran the grocery. Hannah served sandwiches and home-cooked hot meals at the twelve-stool luncheonette counter which adjoined the store.

On Wednesdays, Hannah would serve up roast chicken and her specialty, rice pilaf, an Armenian dish, which consisted of rice, browned orzo noodles, and seasonings. The rice pilaf was a hit.

In 1962, new highway construction was to leave George's stranded on a dead end street. No traffic, no business.

"When the business failed," recalls Hagop Garo ("Jack") Kalajian, "my mother wanted to package the rice pilaf. My father said, 'You can't do that.'"

She did.

With her daughters, Carol and Cohar, Hannah began Near East Food Products, Inc. They would package the rice pilaf and give out samples of the product at local groceries. The three of them would do all the production and packaging by hand and would produce maybe 25 cases a day.

Hannah knew there would be a market demand for her product. Early on, when the luncheonette business still thrived, she received request after request for her rice pilaf recipe. Diners would try to make the concoction at home only to face frustrating results. Hannah, flattered by their unflagging struggle to recreate her culinary artistry, would put up the ingredients in a little bag for customers to take home. It was seat-of-the-pants market research.

Jack Kalajian, now president of Near East Food Products, thinks of himself as a reluctant recruit into his mother's growing business. Hannah had managed to get production up to 150 cases a day by hiring eight women to assist her and her daughters. By 1967, production was up to about 300 cases a day and employees numbered a dozen.

Meanwhile, Jack had gone off to school, become an engineer, and was working nearby in Waltham, Massachusetts. "Seven years into the business, my mother got tired," says Jack, whose face seems to naturally form a smile that says, "Life sure is great. Isn't it?"

In 1967, they were doing sales of $150,000 a year and struggling to make a profit. So Jack agreed to share some of his engineering prowess with Hannah's company. He gave it six months. In that time he designed a simple packaging machine which doubled the amount of rice pilaf that could be packaged in a day without adding any more employees.

Sales grew, but Jack's mom was getting older. She wanted to sell. Jack became president in 1971. While Near East has reached multimillion dollar annual sales (Kalajian is very nebulous about just how "multi"), and there is no question that Jack runs and controls the destiny of the company, it is still very much a family affair. He now owns the company with his two sisters, and his son Eugene is, according to Kalajian, "involved in sales."

"The first thing I did was to look at ways to expand," says Jack. And since the company began with a family recipe, Jack again looked in that direction for new ideas. "Spanish rice seemed to be a popular item. Lentil pilaf was another dish my mother used to serve. I enjoyed both and thought we could sell them." Spanish rice was added to the production lines in 1973 and lentil pilaf was added three years later. In 1973, the company had moved to larger quarters in Leominster, Massachusetts.

But the biggest change in product development probably came in 1973, when Jack decided to impose his personal stamp of eating approval on the product line. "Because of my personal eating habits — I'm into health food — we ate natural foods. I figured if we lived this way, why not do it in the company?"

Natural doesn't necessarily mean simpler, however. Jack met with some resistance when he tried to convince the Nestle company to work with him to develop a bouillon cube he could use in his products that was 100 percent natural. "They said it wouldn't taste good," Jack recalls. "They were right, so we started to experiment. With vegetables, herbs, and other natural flavor enhancers like yeast, which is more expensive than MSG." Ultimately Kalajian insists they came up with a product that tasted even better than it had.

"Quality is number one with ingredients and packaging," Kalajian insists. But Kalajian is not sure that having "100 Percent Natural" stamped on every package of Near East's products helped sales all that much in the beginning. "It was just in the beginning of the era when health foods were coming into favor. The '100 Percent Natural' stamp may have detracted originally, but in the past five years, it's definitely had an impact on our business."

There's no doubt that Near East's business has thrived. In 1977, it broke onto The Griffin Report, a food industry publication, as the 182nd best selling grocery item in Greater Boston. By 1983, it jumped to 7th, ahead of Cheezits, Skippy Creamy Peanut Butter, Chock Full O'Nuts Coffee, Kraft Macaroni & Cheese, and other well-known brand items in the same market. By 1984, Near East had reached 5th on the report, and, they tell me, it is climbing.

Expanding the Product Line

Kalajian doesn't delude himself that the naturalness of his product is the sole reason for success. "All of our competitors are using chemicals and doing quite well," he muses, as he stands to greet Walter Moquin, who has just entered Kalajian's office. Moquin, a former executive with a New England food brokerage firm, came to Near East as vice president for sales and marketing in January 1983. It was a move which signaled Near East's commitment to expanding its product line and moving into a national market.

Thirty percent of Near East's business comes from food service sales, to which it markets three products: Spanish rice, a long grain wild rice blend, and, of course, rice pilaf. There are now a total of eight retail products: rice pilaf, Spanish rice, lentil pilaf, taboule, couscous, sesame tahini, falafel, and wheat pilaf.

"Rice pilaf is probably 40 percent of our total retail sales," says Moquin, who joins in our discussion of Near East's approach to marketing. Moquin is a trim, short man, the type you'd expect toughed it out as a defensive back in college against players twice his weight and height. As consistent as Kalajian's jovial state appears to be, Moquin's serious demeanor is equally as fixed.

"New England is an exceptional area for us," Moquin explains. "The business primarily grew here on rice pilaf. Because rice pilaf is so dominant, it's difficult to achieve the same buying levels for our other products in New England. Outside of

New England, where the market wasn't preconditioned, our products sell fairly equally."

Near East Foods is in the early stages of expanding out of New England and into several other markets, including New York, Philadelphia, Washington, D.C., Florida, and California. "Of our current items, rice pilaf will continue to dominate," Moquin says. "But, outside of New England, we anticipate some of our newer products will at least equal if not exceed its sales."

Product Philosophy Equals Expanded Market Potential

There seems to be a real philosophy behind the development of the Near East products. Kalajian will drop statements like, "I've applied my values for eating habits to the business and make an effort to apply my spiritual values as well." Although you may never really be clear exactly what these "spiritual values" are, you don't doubt him.

As a result, there are certain precepts to keep in mind when talking about the development of Near East products. For instance the company doesn't manufacture boxes of "food"; it creates "carbohydrate substitutes." Boasts Moquin, "There's an integrity to our product." He insists Near East outspends its competitors to create the products.

If Near East's philosophy of carbohydrate substitutes had to be boiled down into a terse "mission" statement, it might be: "The essence of our product is purity, quality, and goodness. Anything short of pure is not good enough for us."

But Kalajian and Moquin are not so naive that they don't recognize the marketing potential of their food philosophy. "Our foods are kosher," says Kalajian. "In fact, they'll be upgraded from K to U, within months."

A "K" indicates that a food is "paraveh," whch signifies that it contains neither animal nor dairy products and therefore can be eaten with either. Under Jewish dietary law, the two are not to be consumed at the same meal. The "U" indicates that the food is

Kosher and has been prepared in accordance with Jewish dietary laws.

"The kosher ratings have a tremendously good impact on our business," notes Moquin. "It shows a real pureness of product."

State-of-the-Art Production Lines

If his spirituality was one important ingredient in Near East's successful product development, so was Kalajian's engineering background. "We probably have one of the most modern, automated plants in the food industry," he boasts. Near East makes its own bouillon and some pasta, and it has just purchased another machine to manufacture macaroni.

The firm also invested in a machine that will make it the only producer of couscous in the U.S. Currently, the product is purchased from France and packaged in Near East's facilities.

Near East has three production lines going 10 hours a day, 4 days a week. The majority of production time is given to packaging rice pilaf, the big seller. The operation goes 4 days a week because Kalajian let his 40 or so employees vote on whether they preferred a 4-day, 10-hour-a-day workweek, or a 5-day, 8-hour-a-day workweek; they chose the former. The original rice pilaf packaging machine that Jack designed for his mom back in the sixties is now being used on a separate line for lower volume Near East products—taboule, wheat pilaf, and lentil pilaf.

Taking Calculated Risks

The purchase of the couscous equipment was a major financial commitment based on Near East's belief that there's enough of a market demand to warrant not relying on overseas production. "People just don't know what to do with couscous," admits Kalajian. "We want to 'Americanize' couscous and tell people how to use it." He'll obviously have to if he expects to make the investment in machinery pay off.

"If the company is really successful, we also make a lot of mistakes along the way. We're really willing to take chances," says Moquin. Kalajian remembers one unquestionable mistake was when he decided to introduce bouillon in liquid form in the sixties, when coffee prices were sharply rising. "We tried it for six months and didn't proceed."

But risks are balanced by conservative moves. Moquin is quick to point out, "We're looking to introduce some more conventional American recipes. Bringing long grain and wild rice to retail, and also introducing chicken and beef rice items." And to the food service side, Moquin confides: "We want to develop an item based on our Spanish rice for Mexican restaurants, because we can really help that industry out." From what he's sampled, the rice offerings at the growing number of Mexican chains could, to be kind, taste better. With their rice pilaf, Near East has already "helped out" such restaurants as Howard Johnson's, Valle's steak houses, and, what has virtually become the landmark of seafood dining in Boston, Legal Seafoods. Moquin is quick to add, "They will also be natural." I wouldn't have thought otherwise.

Turning a Good Idea into a Business

When Jack Kalajian joined his mother's company almost 20 years ago, he was faced with taking what the whole family thought was a good idea and turning it into a business. For a while, the biggest problem was that they couldn't produce the original rice pilaf product fast enough to meet sales demand. With his background in engineering, Jack was able to speed up production and expand product offerings, a feat he is still undertaking.

It's not all that unusual for a family business to undergo major changes when new blood, related or unrelated, is brought in. Perhaps because the new member feels a need to justify his or her addition not just as another family member, but as a boon to the business. Often, as with Kalajian and Near East, the addition breeds enthusiasm which is reflected in product development and ultimately in marketing products to the public. "There's no question we've got the best product anyone could want," Kalajian might say. "All we have to do is get the stuff out there. Peddle our goods agressively."

BANKING ON NEW BLOOD

When Tim Warren joined his family's business in 1973, the business consisted of two independent operations—Warren Publishing Company, which published the weekly *Banker & Tradesman*, a real estate and banking trade newspaper, and Bankers Publishing Company, which published books for bankers. The business was begun by Tim's great grandfather, Willard Clinton Warren, in 1882. In the ensuing century, the business had gone through many forms and moved around between Connecticut, New York, Cambridge, and ultimately Boston, where it is located today on South Street.

It's been a family business since the beginning, with every generation contributing someone to take over the helm. Keith Faulkner Warren, Tim's grandfather who is now in his eighties, acts as the family historian, and several of his reminiscences have been typeset and bound. One brief one, put together in 1982, is titled, *Reflections On A Four-Generation Family Publishing Business.* Here Keith Warren speaks strongly about the concept of the "family business":

"Four-generation family businesses are fairly rare because conditions have to be just right. It presupposes that there are three generations who are willing and able to carry on.

"If the first-generation business shows great possibility for success, the temptation is always to 'go public' or to merge with some other company, in which case, the family may profit greatly from stock ownership but the family no longer is in control and the business is no longer a family enterprise.

"In many respects the family business is similar to the small farms which were handed down from father to son. Alas, this is no longer true.

"Today the person with entrepreneurial instincts develops a profitable idea, forms a company and, once success is fully established, sells out at a good profit and goes onto something else.

"Perhaps the four-generation business, like the small farm, is destined to disappear. I can't help but feel that this would be unfortunate, for the discipline of managing one's own family business gives a sense of personal responsibility which is too often lacking in the executives of larger corporations."

The death knell for family businesses may be a bit premature. Tim Warren, who is slender, bearded, and a diehard Red Sox fan, would like to see his family business grow in profitability. When he came on in 1973, his attention focused on Bankers Publishing Company.

"From 1955 to 1975, Bankers Publishing Company was sort of on the sidelines, not contributing much," Tim says as we sit in his office which overlooks South Station in Boston. "The *Banker & Tradesman* was the thing my father (Tim Sr.) and his father were spending most of their time and energies on."

Bringing a Stagnant Company to Life

Tim's mission when he joined the business in 1973 was to breathe new life into Bankers Publishing Company. His first task was to oversee the production of the seventh edition of Bankers' bread and butter publication, the *Encyclopedia of Banking and Finance.* Since 1924, when Glen Munn wrote the first edition under the editorship of Tim's grandfather, Keith, to the current edition which was completed by F.L. Garcia, the encyclopedia had been the chief contributor to Bankers regular sales.

Although Tim was able to get the encyclopedia revised and Bankers began publishing two books a year, it wasn't until 1981 that the Warrens made the commitment to increase titles from about two a year to somewhere between five and ten a year. "E-7," as they refer to the seventh edition of the encyclopedia, came out in 1974 and seven years later had sold between 11,000 and 12,000 copies. But with all that had gone on with banking legislation during the ensuing 10 years, "E-7" had grown sorely out of date. Tim not only wanted to increase the titles Bankers published, he also wanted an "E-8."

Hiring Experts

Bob Roen had worked with Allyn and Bacon (A&B), a textbook publisher now owned by the Gulf & Western conglomerate, as a managing editor for 12 years. He had been responsible for the acquisition, development, and production of books in A&B's professional division, which published engineering, business, and theatre arts books.

Roen, an editor whose track record at both A&B and Bankers suggests he knows how to acquire marketable titles, remembers, "At the end at Allyn & Bacon, I did everything but education. The mandate when I came here was to acquire and develop a 'reasonable' number of professional books for banks in a year's time. . . . We settled on six titles when I came here. Because Bankers had been producing an average of two books a year for at least the previous five or six years, they didn't feel they could continue through the 1980's at that very slow growth rate."

But his primary task, recalls Roen, whose office boasts two glass-doored bookcases featuring every book ever published by Bankers shelved in alphabetical order, was to deal with the encyclopedia, which was severely out of date. "It was eight years old when I got here. And this was the book that was generating a substantial amount of income for the company."

Roen got the "E-8" manuscript in from Garcia by September 1982. In 1984, it generated 25 percent of Bankers' income. But such a heavy reliance on one book presented problems. At $89, "E-8" is twice the price of other Bankers titles, and it also outsells them two-to-one. Says Roen: "If you have one product that significant to sales, if it starts to decline, you have to replace it with another product equal in value."

Tim Warren is also quick to point out that "We always have a good year when the Encyclopedia gets revised." The numbers seem to bear him out. From 1982 to 1984, when 'E-8" came out, Bankers experienced a growth in gross sales of 150 percent, after it had experienced a drop in 1982.

But "E-8" wasn't the only reason for the large growth in the two-year span. Development of other products was another key ingredient. By 1984, Roen had had a chance to build up Bankers' list of titles. In 1983, it produced five new titles in addition to "E-8." In 1984, six new titles were published.

Roen didn't build up the list alone. Five months after he began, he hired Nancy Long Coleman, an editor with whom he had worked at A&B. Roen scoured journals, trade publications, and banking publications, and he built a network of banking contacts who would keep him abreast of industry trends and areas of concern to bankers. Slowly he built up a list of titles he knew he wanted Bankers to publish.

Cutting Costs to Increase Profitability

He and Coleman worked together to cut production costs and make their books more profitable. They standardized the trim size of the new books so they would all fit into the same size shipping box. No longer would they have to order or stock the myriad sizes and styles of shipping boxes which formerly had to be tailor-made to each book's specifications.

"When I first came," recalls Coleman, who as Bankers managing editor edits, designs, and buys materials for the publications, "I changed the cover material we were using from cloth to leather-like material called 'pyroxylin.'" The cloth cover of a book Bankers had published in 1980 had cost $1.60 per cover, while the pyroxylin cover of a book published two years later cost only $1.26 a book. This represented savings in production costs of more than 20 percent.

Not only did Bankers begin to gain control of costs, it also introduced a system of bidding out typesetting and printing jobs and strict production schedules that gave a clearer idea of when bound books would be shipped to buyers.

"There were few systems in place," Coleman says. "They didn't have a system of bidding out for anything." Once Coleman designs a book in-house, she typically sends it out for price bids to three typesetters. "We don't always go with the lowest bid," she explains. "Schedule and quality are also considerations." While the average price for typesetting a 240-page book runs Bankers around $4,500, prices can range from $3,800 for a simple book to $6,000 for a book with a lot of tables.

Coleman thinks the bidding system they use improves the quality of Bankers' books. "It gives us more control because everyone we work with knows we bid our books out. So we think we get better attention. They try to be fair because they know their bids are being judged in competition with other vendors."

The idea of having schedules beforehand and saying specifically when books would be in was also new to Bankers. Says Coleman; "It was difficult at first for the order processing people to believe that we were really going to have bound books when I said we were going to. They would always tell people it would be three months later, just to be safe. It took a year before they got used to having books on schedule. Bob and I knew we had to prove ourselves to the fulfillment people."

In the last several years, Bankers sales have continued to grow, and each year new products join their growing back list, which, when I talked with them, numbered 29 books. When I asked Tim if he thinks Bankers will ever duplicate the 150 percent sales in growth experienced between 1982-1984, he shakes his head and says, "No." But, he adds, "It's improving the profit margin I'm interested in. Subscription products should improve that."

Introducing a New Product Type

By 1989, Bankers hopes that 50 percent of all new products will be some sort of subscription product. In early 1985, it successfully introduced its first subscription product, a newsletter focusing on lending to small to mid-size businesses. Later in the year it introduced its *Bankers Almanac*, the first in a series of annual publications.

"Subscription products are much more profitable than 'stand-alone' book products," Roen explains. "First of all, subscription products are usually more expensive. In many cases they may be monthly or quarterly, but you get people to pay up-front, so later costs are paid up-front. Subscription products also cost less to sell than 'stand-alone' books because you sell them and automatically ship subsequently. You don't have to resell them.

"With a newsletter, you sell the subscription the first year. If you get 1,000 subs, it's likely 600 will automatically resubscribe. To keep the subscription base at 1,000, you only have to spend enough to get 400 more subscribers. Or you could spend as much as you did the previous year and generate more income by getting 1,600 subscriptions."

As Roen sees it, by the end of 1989, Bankers will have at least two more newsletters, another almanac, and yearly updates for some of its books. "E-8" is scheduled for its next revision in 1988, and Roen would like to do the first annual yearbook for the encyclopedia the following year.

Nancy Coleman is on the phone with one of her suppliers working out a deal to have a forthcoming book printed on the paper that was left over from the "E-8" printing. Her office is set off from the rest of the Bankers' offices, down a hallway which connects most of Bankers' offices to the mailroom and inventory area. All book orders are shipped from this mailroom, using stock that's stored in the inventory room. With current gross sales for Bankers probably between the three-quarter million to one million dollar range, that's a fair amount of stock to keep on hand.

Coleman's office is a very organized version of what a lot of book designer/editor offices look like: desk, work table with light box, a number of design and typesetting books, typestyle sheets hanging on the walls. On one of her walls are a number of clipped cartoons, most of them dealing with publishing or banking. One of them shows a man laughing in a bank as a guard chides, "Please sir, you can laugh all the way to the bank, but once inside you must stop."

When Nancy finishes her conversation and hangs up the phone, I ask her about the new subscription products. While the idea of working on a month-to-month newsletter, which she edits, designs, and sees out the door, is a new experience for her, the prospect seems to keep her excited. Her background is book publishing, where it typically takes at least six months to see a book through to its final stages. Newsletters can turn around in a couple of weeks, which has taken some getting used to.

The *Bankers Almanac*, which was published on the heels of the introduction of Bankers first newsletter, shares a similar design. "The idea is for there to be some product identification on our subscription products," explains Coleman. "Once the customers know the product is good, the almanac will remind them of the newsletter, and they'll buy, buy, buy."

There's no question that Bankers Publishing has changed since Tim Warren joined in 1973. After more than a decade, they are now publishing more books in a more cost-efficient, systematic manner. Tim sees the growth that Bankers is experiencing as "a naturally evolving process."

According to Warren, "Anytime you have new people they have to find something to do. They inject a certain amount of energy into finding things that will support them. The pattern of growth is that you do certain things for a certain amount of time, then you just grow tired of doing those things so you hire someone to do it. You have to justify it with more sales. If you owned a grocery store and grew tired of closing out the register every night at 11 p.m., you have to be able to increase sales to incur the extra expense of covering the salary of someone who's going to close out the register for you."

ABSOLUTELY, POSITIVELY OVERNIGHT

Bankers Publishing Company was already positioned in the marketplace as a publisher of books for bankers. There was a demand for their product. They needed to regularly develop and introduce new products that would meet market needs.

Recognizing a Market Need

Sometimes, however, it takes recognizing the need before the market does. Peter Salisbury, president of Mercury Business Services, developed his company's service based on a need he saw while running the mail room for five-and-a-half years at Ropes & Gray, one of the more prestigious Boston law firms.

"One day on the telephone I heard people bitching about the pricing of Federal Express, mailroom screwups, and bad accountings," Peter tells me in the office suite Mercury rents at One Devonshire Place on Washington Street in downtown Boston.

In December 1983, with $5,000, Salisbury and his brother-in-law, Robert Hodgkins, and their wives formed Mercury Business Services to serve as a middleman in the overnight delivery business. Because Mercury caters to about 35 regular customers, 10 of them every night accounts, they receive a volume discount from Federal Express. They pass some of this discount along to their clients, and they also provide services such as pick-up, filling out airbills, tracing lost packages, and invoicing the day after a package is sent.

Many of the clients are downtown Boston law firms. "Bob developed a program to fill out the airbill," Salisbury says. "Handwritten, they're not readable, but the printout is. We'll fill out the airbills so they go out with a better appearance. We also do all tracing. We're freeing up maybe 10 manhours a day.

"We invoice the next day. The big problem that law firms have is that you send out Federal Express, and the bill comes in two-and-a-half to four weeks later. Then you wait for the mailroom to match up the invoices and to go through disbursements. With a lawyer, if a case is closed, it's closed. You can't bill the customer. That's not the way you stay prestigious."

Salisbury is quick to point out that Mercury is not in any way trying to undermine the quality of Federal Express. In fact, if anything, when they were developing the services, they chose to go with Federal Express because of its excellent reputation for service.

"It's a strange situation," says Salisbury. "The higher ups in Federal Express certainly don't like middlemen or brokers, but they really can't do anything about them. We have the blessing of our sales rep. We're representing their service very well. We don't go in saying we can charge less. We go in saying Federal Express is the best system."

Basically, what Salisbury, Bob Hodgkins, Wendy Salisbury, and Brenda Hodgkins, who still holds a full-time job working with retarded children, are selling is their time. The product they developed is really an add-on service to an already existing product. Federal Express is the basic sound system; Mercury Business Services is the bells and whistles.

In 1984, its first year of operation, Mercury billed a little more than $160,000. In 1985, it expected to bill $400,000 to $500,000, with a 25 percent profit margin.

Distinct Market Positioning

Salisbury holds nothing but optimism for the future of Mercury Business Services. "It's getting to the point where we feel we're going to be the biggest volume Federal Express user in town. No other place does specifically what we do. They don't position themselves the way we do."

Because Mercury will invoice a client the following day, its service is particularly good for third party billers like lawyers, who must turn around and invoice their clients when they receive overnight shipping bills.

Bob tells me, "It's safe to say that the main reason why a law firm doesn't decide right away to go with us is that we sound too good to be true. It's a whole package of saving time and money. If someone's listening and understanding, they can't help but buy our product and service."

Salisbury figures Mercury will save his former employer and current client, Ropes & Gray, more than $50,000 a year that'll come from cuts in such things as overtime, excess package costs, and extra accounting.

"The only negative is if they don't want to let one more set of hands on the paper," Salisbury guesses. "People who don't, don't really understand the mailroom business. If you don't have time to look at the systems, you're not doing your job."

Product development through on-the-job observation is perhaps one way to describe the evolution of Mercury Business

Services. With Salisbury, the evolution came slowly, after years of observing first-hand frustrations in the mail room.

Satisfying Customer Needs

"We can increase a client's discount by at least $2," Bob Hodgkins tells me as he looks up for a second from his computer terminal. "The savings range up to 25 percent. Customers will always save. All of our smaller accounts get a $4 discount on a courier pack. If Federal Express is giving a 15 percent discount, we probably give them 20 percent."

The client base isn't limited to law firms. The night before I met with Mercury, the company had shipped 75 pounds of lobster from a local supplier to a restaurant. For one of its public relations clients, it Fed Ex'd the Boston Celtics' basketball star Larry Bird's sneakers.

Mercury doesn't rely solely on Federal Express. If a client needs to get a package out and delivered the next day,the company will use whatever vendor it has to accommodate the client's needs. "If we have to pay more to use another vendor to keep ourselves looking good, we don't have any problem with that," says Peter.

Meanwhile, Al Felly, who owns the six Felly's Flower shops in Madison, Wisconsin, also tries to satisfy customer needs. So when he recognized that the market needed his flowers, rather than have his greenhouses keep up with sales demand, Felly had them produce as much as they could. "I always said, 'Why don't you grow this much for us?' In reality, at the greenhouse we used to produce less than we needed," says Felly. "Now I tell them to produce as much as they can efficiently and we'll figure out a way to market it."

Because it costs Felly almost the same to grow 100 cases of bulbs as it does 400 cases (28,000 bulbs), his philosophy is: "Produce as much as you can. Put the burden on the market."

R&D: REVELATION & DEVELOPMENT

In 1981, J. Paul Costello, one of the principals in Costello, Erdlen & Co., the Wellesley and Quincy, Massachusetts-based human resource consulting firm, encountered what could best be described as product development through "epiphany experience," a light bulb going off in your head, a "gee whiz" encounter.

The setting was innocuous enough—a Computerland store in Wellesley. "I walked into Computerland four years ago and bought an Apple Computer," Costello tells me as we sit in his Quincy office. One side of the office is plate glass windows which look out at a view of the Boston skyline. A telescope is poised in front of the window. The office is spacious and decorated with heavy leather and wood furniture. Costello himself is well-dressed in a blue suit, with a white handkerchief sticking out of his breast pocket. He's tanned, just having returned from a Florida trip. He looks like you'd expect a "human resource" consultant to look—poised, well-groomed, overall well-packaged. He's also very gadget oriented, attested to by the telescope, the computer video monitor next to his desk, and the fact that because he was slightly late for our morning meeting, he called his secretary from his mobile car phone and asked her to give me the message that he'd be 17 minutes late. His secretary passed on the message making sure to let me know he had called from his car.

Discovering the Product Idea

When Costello bought his Apple Computer he brought it home and started to play with it. "When I saw you could put in a name and a home phone number, my mind exploded," he says. (For the record, not every "epiphany experience" involves mind explosion, but there is precedent. Take, for instance, the experience of the Bible's Paul when he was still Saul of Tarsus and his conversion on the road to Damascus.) While Costello had hardly experienced a religious conversion, he had no doubt that he was on to something significant, something involving major change.

Because he views the employment process as a basic process, Costello had over the years developed a card system to handle the process. "I'd kill clients with the facts if they told me I was doing a lousy job," he jokes.

Saturday became the day Costello and his son would play with the computer. The two Costellos had befriended Lars Perkins, who was working as a salesperson at the Computerland. "Lars recommended stuff to me and became a pal," Costello recalls. A crucial turning point in this product development story came when Lars told Costello he was planning to return to Sweden "because the kids were driving him nuts with joysticks."

For Costello and countless others, the microcomputer was a whole new ballgame in 1981. But Costello thought that if he could develop software based on his card system, they'd blast the human resources market with a product that offered capabilities hitherto unexperienced. Lars at the time was 19 years old, but he and Costello struck a deal and Lars agreed he'd try to design a micro computer system to track resumes.

"We were having a company meeting," Costello remembers. "About 35 or 40 people. I introduced Lars as the person who was going to help us go into the computer business. I announced to our consultants that we were going to develop an automated system."

Lars is now a 25-year-old executive vice president of Micro-Trac Systems, Inc., a subsidiary of Costello, Erdlen & Co. Their list of clients is impressive and includes the Marriott Corporation, Colgate Palmolive, GTE, Pitney Bowes, AT&T Technical Systems, Velcro USA, and Honeywell. The original software developed was the resume tracking system called "ResTrac," which, according to Costello, "is employment as Paul Costello sees it." The cost is $7,995 for a single user and $9,995 for a multiuser. A complete hardware and software system will run between $18,000 and $40,000.

Vertical Marketing

Lars also helped develop "GradTrac," which is a college recruiting model, "AppliTrac," which provides office automation for employment agencies, and "SearchTrac," which provides office automation for executive search firms. The software products, which Costello figures took very little money to develop, showed sales of $500,000 in 1984, and will probably do about $2 million in 1985.

"We're educating the whole marketplace," Costello says. "We designed it for somebody who knew nothing about computers. I'm a wicked gadget person, but I knew nothing about computers. Now I'm a computer freak."

Costello is convinced that vertical software marketing (developing and selling software to be used for specific applications) will be the big thing for the next two years. We walk from Costello's office to the computer room, where there are several IBM PCs, printers, and a Televideo box that is capable of hooking up to eight PCs. Three printers are kept going at once, churning out letters to prospective buyers of the software systems. A thank you plaque from the restaurant chain, "Denny's," hangs on the wall of the room, near a large map of the U.S.

Costello is like a kid in a candy shop in the computer room. While it's clear he doesn't know a lot about programming, nor does he probably need or care to, he loves this room. In fact, he really seems to thrive on developing new products in both the software and human resources consulting divisions of his company.

"The real underlying thing," Costello explains as he sits in front of one of the terminals to show me how simple "ResTrac" is to operate, "is that I don't want to work for anybody. I'm not a great market strategist or anything. I was gone for two weeks. In three days I went nuts. I couldn't wait to get back here. I take five or six vacations a year, but I work seven days a week. I just can't wait to get out of bed to get up and going in the morning."

MARKETING MESSAGES

Philosophy, commitment, enthusiasm — the trilogy of product development and the entreprenueral spirit.

Experiment. Risk failure. — Believe in yourself and your product and the market will follow.

Profit beats volume. — Success is measured in profit margins, not volume.

Chapter Two

Market Research and Product Development: In the Heart of the Market

Al Felly, who runs "Felly's Monona Flowers" out of a green and white aluminum building in Madison, Wisconsin, is something of a local business hero. He gained some national repute as "Mr. Florist" when he tried to launch a national florist service called "1-800-FLOWERS," only to be bought out by two syndicators from Texas after a fairly messy court dispute. Felly's Flowers boasts the largest per-capita flower sales in the nation for a metropolitan area, and it ranked 13th in sales out of all FTD florists in 1984.

Claiming 63 percent of the market in Madison, Felly certainly knows his market and has done his homework. To put it simply, as Felly likes to do, he tells me: "Our whole marketing thrust is that flowers cost too much and don't last long enough. When flowers last longer, they don't cost as much."

His market research is based on first-hand knowledge of his customer. Felly has been selling flowers since he came home to Madison from World War II. During the war, he ran up a bill sending flowers home to a girlfriend. To pay off the bill, Felly worked for a local florist while he was attending the University of Wisconsin. He somehow managed to graduate as an English major with an emphasis on Shakespeare, a graduation he considers to be just short of a miracle. He opened his first store in 1949.

Felly's office is an adventure. In a hutch full of mementos, there's a plaster statue of Elmer Fudd in hunting gear. On a wall behind his desk are various photos, including one of him and his son, Jon, and their catch, a fish larger than the two of them. But mostly the place is cluttered with awards and certificates of appreciation—from the Optimist's Club of West Madison as the Optimist of the Year, from the International Association of Newspaper Advertising Executives for having one of the best 15 advertising ideas in the country, from the Ohio Florist Industry Council on which Felly serves, the first time in their 50 year history, Felly claims, they've elected a "pure retailer" from outside the state.

Systematic market research applied to the development of products and services has been a successful tool for businesses for many years. But there are people like Felly whose market research comes from years of being in the trenches and never letting himself lose sight of what the market wants.

Al Felly gives his customers long lasting flowers at a reasonable price. It sounds simple enough, but Felly says this marketing focus comes not only from direct experience but also includes data available at the university level. "The industry as a whole doesn't have the customer in mind," he explains. This is what sets him apart from his competitors. "Everything we do is concentrated toward the satisfaction of the customer."

It seems to be paying off. Felly says average sales in the flower business were $113,000 per store in 1984. In his Monona store alone, Felly did about $500,000 in sales during the same year. His six stores did around $2.5 million.

Innovation Spells Success

Al Felly believes he's an innovator in the florist industry, and, in all likelihood, he is. He holds a patent on an underwater flower cutting machine which he invented because flowers last longer if they are cut under water.

He also sold manufacturing rights to an open refrigerator display case he developed to Buckbinder, a division of Ardco in Chicago. "There's an evaporative coil which produces a moderately cool temperature and a high humidity," he explains. It runs on 38 cents of energy a day. What we did was to exchange cold, cold temperatures for a very high relative humidity, which is just as important as temperature.

"This is not a keeping tool. This is a selling tool. The hell with keeping it. You want to sell it."

Felly sees himself as a problem solver, and he lectures when he talks to you. When you ask him a question, you might not always get an answer, but there's no doubt you'll get a response. He's also wont to break into one of his "Fellyisms," little words of wisdom or catch phrases which he thinks capture the essence of whatever he may happen to be trying to say.

When he talks about marketing goals, Al tells me: "Flowers are an emotion. I will have achieved my goal when the customer says don't wrap it and is not afraid to carry that emotion and express it. A mature individual is one who takes that handful of happiness and carries it out."

One of the things Al Felly trics to tell me is that customers are responding well to the loose flowers which cost less to make and less to buy. Felly's open case refrigerator helps display the loose cut flowers. In his own way, his market tests prove this is a viable sales option.

Community Reaction, Market Surveys, and Test Markets

There are others whose market research is a bit more elaborate. Gary Scaife, chief executive officer and director of marketing for Natural Choice Industries, Inc., in Westlake Village, California, says that Choice's research for individual products will cost around $25,000 per product. Natural Choice markets fruit juices, including Pink Panther and Sons Pink Lemonade and Juice Drinks and Popeye Punch. The company pays to license the names from MGM/United Artists and King Features Syndicate, respectively.

"We do three basic types of market research," Scaife told me at his Westlake Village office, just outside of Los Angeles. "The first is going into a community to test their feelings to name brands. We'll do a mock-up label and preliminary advertising and promotion.

"Second, we have people who take the products out and do surveys. We try to do at least 2,000 to 3,000 people for each product. Then we go to kids, who are the ultimate consumers. We'll go to soccer and little league games. We have to appeal to their tastes.

"Third, we'll test-market the product in different areas and determine if the response is good. With Popeye Punch we ended up changing the label two or three times and also two of the flavors. The label had to show the fruity aspect of the product, so the name of the product was in different fruity colors, one for each character in the name. It looked good to us. We found out, especially in the Sunbelt, that consumers buy on the look of the product. But there was a confusion to the look. We had to change it so the colors were completely different on each flavor so they could recognize the product."

Give Customers What They Want

Scaife's reaction to his market research findings are very practical. "Unless you're going to spend billions of dollars, you don't educate the public, you give them what they want."

Testing in the Toughest Markets

Near East Foods, Inc., also wanted to see how one of its products, rice pilaf, would sell in one of the toughest markets around, San Francisco, home of Golden Grain, the makers of Rice-a-Roni, the San Francisco treat.

Walter Moquin, vice president of sales and marketing for Near East, says, "It was a test market, but critical because San Francisco was the first market we tested in. We felt it was a true test of the product and the marketing plan. We got a little more than a 6 percent of the San Francisco market in the flavored rice category."

Considering that Moquin's figures place the flavored rice category at $200 million, and Near East's test went head-to-head with one of its more formidable competitors, this first market test elicited enthusiastic responses back at company headquarters. Near East also captured a 6 percent market share in the Los Angeles market.

Knowing How the Customer Thinks

Yet rarely, if ever, does Al Felly face the same kind of competition. Felly is good at what he does because he knows his market and he strives to keep his customers satisfied. Felly's employees seem to enjoy being part of the whole effort. On Felly's desk, which is cluttered with papers and assorted bric-a-brac, is a copy of Lee Iacocca's autobiography given to him by one of his employees. The inscription reads "To Al Felly, for all the good reading material you've given me."

Felly has a list of required reading for his managers. It's largely a smattering of business and management books, but there is also material focusing on Abraham Maslow's theories of behavior. Maslow believes that the "needs for safety, belongingness, love relations and for respect can be satisfied only by other people ...." Felly's people give the customer the respect and, in a certain sense, the "safety" they need when they walk into a Felly's Flower store.

The reading material is supposed to help the managers not only understand how businesses work, but also how their customers think.

Using Available Market Research

Nothing is really a small project for Felly. His research and implementation have infused a great deal of innovation and progress into the florist industry, an industry which Felly says, doesn't always move as swiftly as it might.

"Preservatives have been around for years," Felly explains. "But only 27 percent of our industry uses preservatives today."

Felly and I walk upstairs in the Monona "complex" to a conference/training room, which Felly rents out to businesses and also uses to conduct his own seminars. We view some of the videotapes of ads he's run, and listen to cassettes of radio ads. He plays with a tape recorder that is capable of speeding up the message, but still keeps it understandable. "I can acquire speed listening," Felly tells me. "I can listen to an hour tape in 45 minutes." Everybody in business should own one, he says.

At first I wonder why anyone would want to increase the speed at which they listen to things; but then again, here's a man who's been at his desk since five-thirty on the morning of a major snowstorm. Felly can't get enough information.

"We're using a different post-harvest care method, trying to see which method is the best," Felly explains, showing me a table full of carnations in vases of various solutions, which sits on the stairwell outside the conference room. Sunlight shines through the plateglass above and surrounding the stairwell. "I hope we never get to the point where we're not constantly looking for a better way."

Felly experiments with everything that comes in. Recently, a lot of his experimentation focuses on the use of STS (silver thiosulfate) as a preservative. "Wild aster — you pick it and within hours it dies," Felly tells me back in his office. "That particular flower reacts enormously well to STS solution. With the solution it lasts two to three weeks.

"Ethylene triggers mechanisms of the flower," Felly continues. "Practically everything we cut we experiment with to see if we can break the triggering habit. We've taken snapdragons that'll normally last two to three days and have them living for a month."

"We've just had a major breakthrough," Felly tells me. "STS when used by itself has a tendency to attach to a flower's cell walls. By using 8HQC and an acidifier (citric acid) you can lower the flower's pH.

"Part of the experiment we're doing upstairs is something called 'sugar loading,' a 10 percent sugar solution for 24 hours. We're looking at the possibility of 60-day carnations."

Marketing Potential of Research

Felly is quick to point out the marketing potential of such a finding. "During April, a low sales period, we might be able to purchase flowers here, put them in solution, and sell them in May. With a 60-day carnation, you can still assure the customer of two to four weeks."

"You want to know how to get your flowers to last longer?" Felly asks, like someone who offers you the key to picking a winner at the track. "Mix half tap water and half 7-Up or Sprite, or any clear soda pop containing citric acid and sugar. That'll give you certainly double the life of your flowers." Felly has just given me the same basic formula that the company is experimenting with in its 8HQC and acidifier solution, sugar loading.

Felly offers to drive me back to my hotel. As we're driving away from the Monona store, we talk some more about his Felly's Flowers market research, product development, as well as its general approach to the market.

"I find Felly's Flowers an amazing business for a tiny business in some of the things we've done," he says. Later, as he pulls the car over to drop me off, he throws in one last Fellyism, which pretty much explains to me why tomorrow he'll be back at his office at five-thirty in the morning: "The true satisfaction in life is climbing the mountain and finding there's a bigger mountain on the other side."

MARKETING MESSAGES

The Three-Step Solution to meeting market needs: Information (plus) Persistence (plus) Innovation (equals) Success.

Know your market and give it what it wants.

Always look for the best way to deliver the goods.

Chapter Three

Where Quality Controls

Hudson, New Hampshire, is a dot-on-the-map of a town with the usual faceless industrial parks and strip shopping centers. Its only real tourist attraction is Benson's Wild Animal Park. When I stopped at the local convenience mart/newspaper stand to buy *The Wall Street Journal*, the manager said he carried only one copy and every day the same customer comes in to buy it. Yet it is here, in the obscurity of Hudson, that Paul Villemaire based his AMF Industries, Inc., in 1978. In 1981, AMF reported $3 million in sales; three years later, AMF had done over $22 million. In early 1985, Villemaire changed AMF's name to Hudson Industries, Inc.

Hudson is a holding company for four divisions: American Metal Fabricators, a sheet metal manufacturing house; Mechanical Assembly, which assembles cabinets for various industries, but mostly for the computer industry; C&M Screw Machine Products; and Hawk Electronics, begun in late 1984 as an assembler of electronic cable and cable harnesses.

Quality Keeps Customers

Quality control is one of the factors that has contributed to Hudson Industries' substantial growth over the past few years. Villemaire, a large, hulking man with a thick brown moustache and perpetual grin, tells me they had some of their best growth years during the recession of the early 1980s.

"Through the recession years, 81, 82, and part of 83, the downturn years, we started working on quality," Villemaire tells me as we sit in his office with his general manager, Armand Carpentier, and Dave Bascom, his quality control manager. "We doubled in size each year due to the quality of our products. People began weeding out the poorer shops and giving work to the shops with quality. In the Greater Boston area, there are probably about two dozen good shops. These shops will grow with the big customers. People out there simply trying to make a week's pay will always be making it, but not with the Digitals and Wangs."

Digital and Wang do a lot of business with Hudson. For Wang, American Metal Fabricators fabricates a great deal of hardware, including thousands of the metal "birdcages (more than 90,000 to date)," the part of the computer that the disks will ultimately fit into. The Mechanical Assembly Division buzzes constantly as assembly lines fit together products ranging from Digital's VAX/11780 and Unibus Cabinet to Wang's Meg-80 Cabinet and VS-15 Cabinets. For an onlooker who's passing by, it's amazing enough that they're able to tell the difference between any of the products they're assembling, let alone have quality ratings of 98 percent-plus.

Inventory Cost Controls

"The driving force behind tightening up quality control," Villemaire tells me, "was being inventory conscious. We're trying to look through a narrower window, trying to turn around the product much quicker. Companies can't afford an inventory problem. If they need parts, they can't afford to have the part rejected because the lines will run out of parts. If they have to hedge quality and need to bring it in two weeks ahead, that causes inventory problems.

"Today, with the cost of money so much higher, inventories play a big part of profits. Digital has a $2 billion inventory with $5 billion in sales. Technology changes so quickly with new products coming on line that there's an obsolescense of inventory. Instead of tossing $2 or $3 million worth of inventory down the tubes, they try to maintain inventory at low levels."

Establishing Overall Standards

Dave Bascom has 20 years of experience in the manufacturing end of the sheet metal business. In 1982, Villemaire hired him to establish overall quality control standards for all of Hudson Industries. "Prior to Dave coming on board, production really did quality control," says Villemaire. "When Dave came on, it became a stand alone department."

Bascom, a Hudson native, is a tall, balding man, who has an interesting habit of referring to Villemaire as "Paul" when he's in the room with him, and "Mr. Villemaire" when he's not. "The number one reason our quality control program has worked," Bascom says, "is that Paul has always backed me up. You can make up all the standards, but if you don't have the backing of the number one man, it doesn't amount to anything. It's unique in this industry that I only have to go through Paul. I get a decision in five minutes, not three weeks. Things can get rolling, done. That's a big asset."

"Just-in-Time" Delivery

Tied in with the obsession with controlling inventory costs, Hudson Industries is looking at "just-in-time" delivery, which means they are aiming to deliver plus-or-minus one day of the due date. This is an incredibly tough goal for people in the industry to reach. "We're working with Digital who's in the forefront of delivery," Armand Carpentier tells me. "Paul's made a commitment that we'd be their first plus-or-minus one day deliverer."

Bascom adds: "Instead of shipping early, we'll now keep a product on our shelves and deliver it just in time. We see it as a reality. It's not that outlandish, but a matter of tighter controls. We already have our standards down pat."

At a recent meeting that Digital had for its vendors, Bascom says that other vendors shook their heads at the plus-or-minus one day idea. "Digital asked me if I thought it was outlandish," he says. "I said, 'No. As a matter of fact, we're doing it now'," a comment that no doubt made Bascom extremely popular with the other vendors.

Jump in Quality Ratings

One of the reasons Villemaire hired Bascom was because of Bascom's manufacturing background. "In our type of organization you need someone with a manufacturing background," he says, confirming that his boss made the right decision in hiring him. "People with just a quality control background, it's too easy to bull them. It's pretty tough to put a guy with a background just in quality control in there telling manufacturing what's wrong with the plant."

The difference that the Hudson Industries' commitment to quality has made is evidenced by quality ratings from Digital which have jumped from 80 percent to a formal quality control program to 98 percent-plus now.

"Competitors are getting to be in awe of us," Bascom tells me. "We have a super name in the marketplace. A close friend of mine who is the general manager for Brockhouse, in Exeter, asked me, 'What are you guys doing over there?' No matter who I talk to our name is coming out of their mouth."

Getting Back to Quality

Villemaire is amazed at how far quality control has come since his days as a purchasing agent for Digital, where he worked for 11 years, having worked his way up from a $2.50-an-hour job as a wireman.

"Back then it was mostly a gut feeling. They didn't have the documentation," he explains. "Quality in the past wasn't the issue. Years ago it was important, but it deteriorated. Now companies like Chrysler are going back to quality. Their five-year, 50,000 mile warranty shows a different industry reverting back to corporate quality control.

"With the computer industry, now that competition is there, they have to produce quality. They now look at the real cost to get a customer and say 'Poor quality costs us money.' The used to say 'We can buy it for $10 from AMF or $9.50 from XYZ.' Now they go with us because they don't want to deal with poorer quality."

The tight quality standards initially caused some strain between Hudson Industries and some of the businesses they subcontract plating or other work to. "We went through a period when we had such tight quality control that they refused to do work," Villemaire recalls. Bascom chimes in, "Paul said, 'Fine, pull their work.' Within three weeks they were back meeting our specifications because we were supplying 80 percent of their work."

"We felt if they were going to do business with us, they'd do it on our terms," Villemaire adds. "It's not good enough for us unless it's right."

The Psychology of Quality Control

There's also a very practical reason to be super-cautious with quality standards. "If we're keeping tighter control than the customers are asking for," says Bascom, "then even if we miss something, hopefully we'll pass Digital's inspection. We have a high 90s rating in mechanical assembly with Digital because our standards are tighter than what they're asking for."

Sometimes it's not just the quality, but the quality plus a little psychology that pays off. Says Villemaire: "I remember when we first started, I spent a lot of money on special packaging. You don't package it properly, it gets damaged. You've got to do it again anyway. If it looks good, the inspector looks for the good. If it looks bad, you're asking for rejection. The inspector says, 'What a mess. What's wrong with this?'"

The obsession with quality runs rampant at all of Hudson's divisions. Roger Martin, president of the C&M Screw Machine Products division, told me earlier, "Last year we did over four million parts for Wang. The quality control rating was around 99.7 percent." He added the obvious: "Business has grown by word of mouth."

Robert E. Breton, general manager of the mechanical assembly division, boasts: "No one in the industry has our facilities, buying power, workforce, or knowledge."

Dennis Sylvester, president of American Metal Fabricators, who has been with Villemaire since the beginning, says: "We're probably the most soundly structured company for this type of work that you're ever going to walk into. We have a 12-man quality control department, 10 in-process inspectors, one final inspector, and a manager. You won't find that in any other sheet metal shop. You won't find the quality control equipment we have in other sheet metal companies. We give the customer what he wants and them some."

And Jack Metzemaekers, president of the newly formed Hawk Electronics (Hawk is said to be one of Villemaire's nicknames because of any icy stare, a "hawk gawk," he is capable of), has invested heavily in the latest quality control equipment for the electromechanical division.

"We bring people around to our facilities and then to Dave's quality control room," Armand explains. "Dave does a dance on their heads. When you pull out six months of 100 percent ratings at Digital, it's hard to question somebody's credibility. Anyone can say, 'We have 99.5 percent ratings,' but when you physically show them documentation, it's hard to question."

Dave Bascom's office is in the same building in the industrial park which houses American Metal Fabricators. Hudson Industries occupies five of these buildings, but the company is in the process of building a larger structure, which, in addition to substantial warehouse space, will house the corporate offices. Bascom's current office has no windows. Its decor and furnishings are stark. A metal desk with plenty of file drawers holds his papers. He opens his file, places reams of paper in front of me, and begins his "dance of documentation."

Quality Control Documentation

The figures are impressive. A November 1984 quality rating from Wang for a product American Metal Fabricators is producing is 94 percent. For the period between December 1983 and November 1984, there is a year-to-date rating of 91.46 percent.

There's also a letter from Gould Inc., of Andover, Massachusetts, explaining that its rating system is on 4-point basis. If you have two months below a 3.0 rating, Gould takes "corrective action." After three months below 3.0, you're disqualified from any further purchase orders. "We have a 4.0 rating from Gould," Bascom tells me. "No rejects."

"I also know it's about a 98.5 percent rating with Wang while they only report it as 94 percent. Half the time, when our quality rating is less than 100 percent, we can substantiate it. We really are about 99 percent-plus accurate. The times when we're not, they'll usually substantiate that there's a quirk in their systems. But the thing is they don't correct it in the documentation. There's no method to correct it as of now."

Bascom keeps extensive paperwork flowing to keep customers aware of the commitment to quality. "For Digital, we have a vendor sponsor in Burlington, Vermont," he says. "Every month I go down through the documentation with him. I put out a memo to him stating the items that are Digital's responsibilities. I do that monthly, even though they don't take it off our report card. At least there'll be a note on the report. Our sponsor asks me why I don't just send in a report every six months. I respond, 'No, this way it's fresh.' I want it right up-to-date."

State-of-the-Art Quality Control Equipment

Even the quality control equipment is right up-to-date. "In my first six months," Bascom tells me, "I told Mr. Villemaire that I needed $50,000 worth of equipment. He said, 'If you need it, get it.'"

So Bascom did. In the main quality control room of American Metal Fabricators, not far from his office, he shows me some of his acquisitions: A Hansford Rapid Check, which measures within 1/10th of a thousandth of an inch the width of an object cost $37,000; a Brown & Sharpe Micro-hite, which measures height eight times faster that a manual height gauge (which costs $700) cost $17,000. "You won't see this at every shop," Bascom boasts.

As we walk through this main quality control room, Bascom tells me, "My inspectors are mechanics. They should be able to go out and build any part."

Ship-to-Stock Status

Bascom walks me through the main shop area toward the final inspection room, explaining as we go that every piece of material that comes in the door is thoroughly inspected before it gets used. He also tells me that none of the firm's competitors have as large a "ship-to-stock" ratio as they do, which means that rather than a customer feeling the need to have an inspector come down to the shop and inspect the pieces, they can be shipped directly and placed right on the inventory shelves. That's how good Hudson's quality rating has become.

Final Inspection

We enter the final inspection room, where Don, the final inspector, is manning the helm. The room is air conditioned in the summer. "Source inspectors from the companies we supply fight to come here. Everything's here," Bascom says, pointing at the equipment neatly arranged around the room. "If he needs any equipment, it's right there."

In the final inspection room, Don, or whoever is on as final inspector, looks for problems that the floor inspector might have noted. The final inspector's job is to make sure that the problems are corrected. He also sends items out for a finish if they need one, and tests the finish to make sure it is correct by using a gloss meter. Don patiently shows me how the gloss meter works; he says that Wang and Digital are quite insistent that the finish on their products is what they want and not something near what they want.

Getting specifically what they want is obviously important to many of Hudson's customers. Dennis Sylvester, president of American Metal Fabricators, told me, "We do a lot of specialized fixtures that give a customer the assurance of quality." One such "specialized fixture" is a vise used to make a Wang 80-Meg Cabinet. The vise looks like a small metal table with various protrusions at strange angles. It cost American Metal Fabricators $8,000 to make, according to Sylvester. "We've sent out 1,500 cabinets and had no returns," he says. "It makes me money up front for each one." Obviously, it is quality money well spent.

"We're Digital's number one sheet metal vendor and Wang's number two sheet metal vendor," Bascom tells me as we walk by sheet metal presses. But I know something more is coming, because admitting you're number two so pleasantly is not part of Bascom's quality dance. He explains: "We are a 'soft tooling' sheet metal house. We do everything by hand. A 'hard tooling' house makes up a die. Once Wang or Digital accepts hard tooling, there's no more rejects. "Wang's number one vendor is a hard tooling house. That's why we're their number two sheet metal vendor."

Quality Over Price

Quality control is integral to Hudson Industries' marketing success. The kind of clients it deals with, in fact, are more often concerned with quality than with price. What good is a product, even if it's cheaper, if the quality's so bad you can't use it?

Hudson's commitment to quality has also seen them quite nicely through tough economic times. When its customers cut back, they cut back on the vendors who can't make the grade.

In Hudson, New Hampshire, where it's tough to get a *Wall Street Journal* unless you subscribe, or beat the guy who gets it every day to the convenience mart, Paul Villemaire is producing and Dave Bascom is choreographing quite a show of sophisticated, successful quality control. With quality ratings from its customers of 94 percent and above, it's fairly safe to say they've opened to rave reviews and promises of a long run.

MARKETING MESSAGES

Quality is the halo of your reputation. Make it shine.

Quality counts often more than price.

When the going gets tough, quality gets going. Nothing succeeds like success.

Maxim Two

The Entrepreneurial Difference

I am what you are...
but I'm better.
In a sea of similarity,
make your product stand out.

So you've got the product. With more than one-half million businesses beginning each year, there's bound to be some pretty tough competition.

What are the entrepreneurs out there doing to make sure they're not swallowed up by someone who might be offering a slightly shinier mousetrap or new and improved soapflakes? Are they cowering in the wake of an impending marketing doom? Of course not.

The people who succeed let the buying public know their product or service is better than a similar product or service down the road. Their diner serves better burgers. Their condominiums are more luxurious. Their specialty shop is more special.

The better businesspeople I spoke with, in terms of success *and* reputation, believe in what they're marketing and convince the public that they, too, should believe. They're not trying to dupe the public by selling what is essentially the same product at perhaps a higher price. By taking the time and care to package their products creatively they truly are in many instances giving the buying public a "better" black box. By differentiating their products or services just enough to add that little bit of extra value, these entrepreneurs truly are giving the consumer a little more bang for the buck. By using creative selling techniques, perhaps a diner film series or a special Halloween promotion at a specialty shop, the buying experience is made more delightful.

The businesspeople I met who are successfully convincing the marketplace that their wares are better take the time and use innovation and creativity to make their products stand out from the crowd. They're successfully marketing products to an evermore discriminating marketplace. They're excited by being perceived as different, often better, in that marketplace. The excitement infuses them with the energy to continue making their products shine.

Chapter Four

Packaging: Eat at Ed's 'Cause You Can't Bowl There

From the outside, Ed Debevic's Short Orders/Deluxe looks like packaging pure and simple. A closer look reveals something more. Behind the glow there is quality food and quality service. And Ed's, open only three months at the time of my visit to Chicago, is a success in a city known for its excellent restaurants.

Though it is a diner it has become the local place to be. Fur coats mingle with Barracuda jackets; Mercedes park next to Ford Escorts, making Ed's a cause celebre—diner chic. Ed's is consistently packed. It's probably the only diner with valet parking. A giant Coca-Cola bottle is posted to a large pole at the end of Ed's parking lot. On the building itself a large banner gets straight to the point: "Get In Here."

Packaging a Concept

Most people when they think of packaging think of the box the corn flakes come in, or those pretty little boxes that drive the cost of Godiva chocolates even higher. With Ed's we're talking more abstractly. Ed's is a prime example of the packaging of a concept—the dream diner. The diner you remember from your childhood. The one that never really existed. What good is packaging a diner concept unless it's the best diner you ever set foot in? Ed's is the diner you always dreamed of, but never knew.

I walk into Ed's at eleven-thirty in the morning on a Friday. There's already a 25-minute wait for lunch. "At The Hop" is playing on the jukebox as middle-class housewives corral their children to wait in line behind gray-suited businesswomen and men. There's a plate glass window to the display kitchen, where burgers are being ground and pattied and a sign that says, "If you find a better diner, eat there." A large plastic cow, named "Burmingham Collins III," stands inside the window of the display kitchen. There's also a display case with rows of fresh burger patties, chicken breasts, baking potatoes, oranges, and red sweet peppers. A vision of loveliness to almost any food lover.

Ed's is the brainchild of Rich Melman and his Chicago-based company, Lettuce Entertain You Enterprises, Inc. Lettuce Entertain You restaurants do about $40 million a year in sales. Collins Food International, a Los Angeles-based publicly held company, which is also a major franchise of Sizzler Steak Houses and Kentucky Fried Chicken restaurants, went in as a partner with Melman, putting up a good deal of the money to get Ed's going. Melman estimates that the overall bankroll to get the place open ran about $1.2 million. Lee Cohn, a friend of Melman, is also a partner in Ed's. Cohn has his own restaurant business in Phoenix called "Big 4."

Michael Jaye, director of public relations and promotions for Lettuce Entertain You, walks in and guides me to a booth. Michael explains the partnership with Collins Foods and Lee Cohn. "Ed's is a partnership," he says. "We opened one in August of 1984 in Phoenix, prior to the opening of this one in

November. It's doing well in Phoenix, but the market's not the same."

Bill Raffel, an executive vice president with Smith, Badofsky & Raffel, Lettuce Entertain You's advertising firm, joins us. He and Jaye proceed to talk about all the plans for promotions and advertising they made, but never had to use. Ed's took off without any advertising, the day it opened.

Melman slides into the booth to join us. He is a boyish looking man, with a Dutch-boy haircut. Since the early 1970s, starting from virtually nothing, his success as a Chicago restaurateur has been from all accounts legendary. His most recent coup was being hired to redesign the Playboy Clubs.

Product, *Service*, Then *Packaging*

"I was out in Phoenix talking about the trend in American food," Melman explains when I ask him how Ed's was conceived. "We started laughing about American food—macaroni and cheese, meatloaf, burgers and malts." During the discussion he hit upon the idea of Ed's, the dream diner.

"The product is always the most important thing," Melman insists. "Then it's service. Then it's packaging. If you have all three, it's great. I get real neurotic and keep jumping from area to area until we improve. My greatest strength is putting together a good team and knowing what I need."

Raffel adds: "Rich has phenomenal attention for detail. The booths on the different levels don't match to give the feel that Ed's grew little by little as Ed got more money."

Ed Debevic doesn't really exist, of course. Melman, Lee Cohn, Raffel, and others created him. They even gave him a detailed history and designed the diner to reflect it. There's a counter that was supposedly the original diner. There are two levels of booths, each with a different color formica and naugahyde to indicate they weren't built at the same time. There's a porch where two television sets play soap operas, which in the din of the crowd couldn't possibly be heard. There's also a banner which reads, "Welcome Home Ed, We Missed You." Ed, it seems, was a Korean War vet.

An afternoon in Ed Debevic's is a sensory overload. So much color, so much detail, so much jukebox, so much . . . Ed. By the time you leave, you know him. Ed's your buddy.

The packaging is perfect. You want to get inside and eat up as much of this dreamworld as you possibly can. Melman smiles when talking about how well the place is doing.

"Collins Foods put in most of the money. Everybody seems pretty happy with the return right now. I'm not saying specifics, but the Collins people are smiling. Maybe I shouldn't be that flippant," he says, catching himself gloating a bit. On normal average weekdays and Sundays, Ed's will service around 1,500 people. On Saturdays, the number doubles. The average meal ticket runs a meager $6. Melman has reason to gloat.

Customer Input, Instincts, and Flexibility

The evolution of Ed's owes much of its development to seat-of-the-pants marketing know-how.

"The best thing I do," Melman says, "is talk to customers and listen to them. That to me is what all these high-falutin market surveys are all about. Our customers often tell me the marketing terms. They tell me what I'm doing.

"It's instinct. We look around. We travel. Business is not exactly a science. In chemistry, hydrogen and oxygen always equal water. In business, there are certain principles combined with instinct and flexibility—no guarantees. You drive yourself crazy thinking about whether everybody else will like this place. You hope you remain in the mainstream. You don't want to be driving a Rolls and eating caviar because sometime you might forget and begin to think everybody lives like that."

For a lot of the development of Ed's, sophisticated market research wasn't needed. Häagen-Dazs ice cream is served in the chocolate malts, not because it's expensive, trendy, or because research results demanded it, but because Melman thought it tasted better than any other brand.

"We talked to our moms and our friends and got old recipes," Melman explains. "The meatloaf came from my partner Lee's wife's grandmother Hortense's recipe," he claims, although later someone else claims it was really Ed's cook's mother's recipe. It's not really important where the recipe came from, as long as it was from somebody's mom.

Melman and Raffel begin a discussion of the cherry pie.

"Is that really gummy?" Melman asks.

"Sort of gelatinous," Raffel answers.

"I didn't like it the last time. They said they were changing the recipe for the filling," Melman says, taking a forkful of Raffel's pie. He nods approval.

I bring up a review I ran across in the *Chicago Tribune* which said that Ed's is important without having important food. "It is important," Melman insists. "What's important? People like it. It may not be 'chi chi' food that's been around for a long time, but I couldn't give up hamburgers."

The 80 Percent Rule

"You know, it's just one of those things, this place," Melman explains. "The highest I ever get in knowing a place will work is 80 percent. Ed's was an 80 percent. I felt good about this place, but I still called my wife and asked her to have some friends come down on opening day, just in case. An hour-and-a-half after opening, we were mobbed." Melman says he's been lucky. "I've never opened one up that didn't take off."

Ed's certainly takes a prize for its relaxed, informal atmosphere. In the next booth a young lady is having a birthday party, which is made clear by a parade of waiters who have formed a cha-cha line and are now dancing their way to her booth. "How old are you?" a waiter asks as he places a brownie decorated with a candle in front of her. "Don't get worried, you'll get married someday," a waitress assures her, after they've given her a rousing chorus of "Happy Birthday." Over the speaker, a voice says, "Hey Erin, Beth says 'hi'," and "Blue Moon" begins playing on the jukebox.

"The bottom line," Melman says, "is being able to tell what you need. I'm pretty good at being able to analyze. This became the hot restaurant in town the day it opened in 1984."

As Melman gets up to leave with Michael Jaye and Bill Raffel, he tells me: "I'll cooperate with you 1,000 percent if you promise not to just play up Rich Melman, but rather give credit to all these people who are responsible."

Actually, it's Ed who will be "played up." Melman and his team have done such a thorough job packaging this concept that Ed is almost real. He's the star. As Melman told a reporter from the *Chicago Sun-Times* before Ed's opened, "We have a sense of Ed, so we don't get too carried away."

Micky West, one of two general managers, takes me around to see the sights. West has been in the restaurant business 14 years. He's had four of his own places, where he even did his own cheffing. "I'm from Milwaukee," West confides. "So Ed's is home for me. This is like fine dining in Milwaukee."

Currently Ed's is opened from eleven in the morning to midnight, Monday through Thursday, until one in the morning on Saturday, and until ten at night on Sunday. West tells me there are plans to begin opening for breakfast. Oatmeal and ice cream, West tells me, will be one of the big items.

Everybody's Part of the Package

"Overall, the staff here is a lot happier than in a normal restaurant because of the atmosphere," says West. "It's not like a regular restaurant where you have the front of the house and the back of the house. Here, cooks have a lot more fun. Everybody's part of it. They're on display.

"We have a structured program as far as service, but the waitresses' personalities are up to them. As long as they fit into the

Ed's concept, how much hamming it up they want to do is up to them."

On the Sunday before my visit, the *Chicago Tribune Sunday Magazine* ran a story on Ed's which played up the meatloaf special. "Since that article," West explains, "we've had 140 orders of meatloaf in one day. At one point we were out of it for over an hour."

Ed's menu has not been without its items that bombed. Ring bologna (a knockwurst-like lunch meat) and smoked butt bombed, according to West, who adds, "If my servers are sold on selling it, it'll sell." West points to a sign that reads, "If you were a really good customer, you'd order more."

In front of the display kitchen West explains that Ed's meat is prepared from scratch. "We grind the chuck in the sight of the guest, and display it so they can see it. All we use is chuck roast. All the patties are used within four hours. Every two trays (there are 73 patties per tray) is gone within an hour. We grind enough patties at night to make it through the first hour of lunchtime the following day."

Another sign announces, "You are looking at burger history in the making."

At the other end of the counter from the display kitchen is Michael Bukitus, Ed's "crazed baker." He's responsible for prepping and baking more than 1,000 buns a day, plus all other baked goods in the place, which, judging from the giant chocolate-covered donut which hangs from the ceiling, includes chocolate-covered donuts. "We sell about 150 hamburgers an hour," West says. "So 13 or 14 dozen buns can go in an hour."

Somedays Ed's sells 900 shakes and malts, West explains as we move to the malted area, just off the bakery. "All one guy does is make 9-ounce portions of ice cream scoops for the malteds. Another guy just makes malteds." I see the guys in question. They're pros.

The "Diner Hall of Fame," is one wall of Ed's which is plastered with autographed photos of waiters and waitresses from actual Chicago restaurants. Most of the people in the photos have the kind of faces that would give a casting director for a Fellini movie a field day. One of the waitresses pauses as she passes us, points to a picture of an elderly waitress and says, "That there's my idol."

Nearby is Ed's bowling case. "There's no first place trophy," West apologizes. "Ed wasn't a real good bowler." A Brunswick Black Beauty undrilled 16-pounder sits in the center of the bottom shelf.

We pass a sign, "The more you tip, the nicer we are." Near the restrooms there's a wall of photos with a sign above, "Places To Go In Chicago." The pictures include bathrooms at Wrigley Field and Shedd Aquarium, as well as the players' dressing room at Comiskey Park. In another area of the diner six bowling balls are embedded into the wall; each is labeled with Ed's high score for six years during the 1950s. The scores range from 250 to 270. "They got a little carried away," West smiles. "I don't think he ever bowled that high."

The men's room is immaculate. There's a vending machine which, among other items, sells Alka-Seltzer and prophylactics. A sign over the mirror reads, "No wonder you're going home alone."

"Nothing here is technically that hard to do," West explains as we finish our tour. "But it's hard to do it all right. We pay a lot of attention to detail."

As I leave, I notice the bowling game machine up front, plus a case full of "Ed Debevic's Beer," a special brew made up for Ed's. "Ed's is one of the few places you can get hamburgers and Amaretto," Bill Raffel had joked earlier.

In the parking lot the attendant gets my car which is parked near a Jaguar, a Mercedes convertible, and a Jimmy 4X4 truck.

As I drive away from Ed's, the Chicago public radio station plays, "Let's Have Another Cup of Coffee." Before I finish my stay in Chicago, I know I'll be back at Ed's with friends doing just that.

Marketing Messages

Packaging makes your product shine. The successful entrepreneur knows, however, that it's no substitute for having the best product.

If you want to know what the market likes, ask. Listening to customers is a sure way to tailor your packaging. Let the customer design the important details for your market.

Remember the 80 Percent Rule. Never be certain of more than 80 percent of anything in business. That way you'll always be ready with backup plans, just in case.

Chapter Five

Product Differentiation: Humble Arrogance in the Marketplace

"There's rarely market research in real estate," Merrill Diamond tells me as we sit in the Brookline, Massachusetts, office of Parencorp, a real estate development company Diamond owns with his partner, Gordon Hurwitz. "Marketing's usually a reaction to get the bank to give you money."

In a city full of real estate developers, Parencorp has certainly managed to set itself apart since it was formed in 1977. Parencorp, which draws its name from Diamond and Hurwitz's wives *(Pa*ula and Ka*ren)*, grew out of the architecture firm of Hurwitz/Diamond, which began in 1973 and still exists, but only to service the architectural needs of Parencorp. "Our profits as architects in some years were tens of thousands, in a good year maybe hundreds of thousands. Now profits are in the millions," says Diamond.

Diamond is clearly the talker of the company. After spending five minutes with Hurwitz and Diamond, Hurwitz gets up and excuses himself to leave by saying, "He'll tell you all my secrets." Perhaps they're not secrets, but Diamond does proceed to tell me his formula for making his product stand out as different in the marketplace.

"We are perceived in the marketplace as being very different. The work we do is as unique as our marketing approach. But so few developers pay attention to marketing that if anybody does anything, it stands out," says Diamond, who is an interesting study in contrasts. "Humble arrogance" was an oxymoronic phrase once used to describe former President Jimmy Carter. Diamond, with his knack for building himself up while at the same time bragging how it didn't take anything special to succeed, fits the phrase perfectly.

Thought, Creativity, and Marketing Lures

"Some of my friends who are developers have great projects but don't think of how best to market the project," Diamond continues. If it's on a river they'll name it "Riverview." No thought, no creativity to try to induce somebody to buy, he insists.

"That's going to change. I'm going to make it change."

Parencorp is positioned as a company that does unique, quality work. It also does expensive work. Diamond's first glimmer of marketing prowess came when Parencorp was the developer for an old Wheelock College dormitory in Brookline. Diamond did a little legwork and found that the house had been built by a member of the Sears family, an old Boston family. While no one in the Sears family lived there for any duration, it gave Diamond a hook.

"I realized we could get more billing it as the Sears Estate," Diamond says. "Now it's even on Boston walking tours. We had John Sears out for the opening and he told me that of all the buildings associated with the Sears', this is the last one he would have thought of. But Isaac and Frances Sears had built it. Two or three years later, their shoe business burned down and they moved out. No Sears has been connected with it since."

By making the Sears Estates "historic," Diamond was able to differentiate these condominiums they were developing and selling for $300,000 to $400,000 per unit in 1982. "I figured I'd go after a Back Bay market. I figured if I could get people from the Back Bay, they wouldn't think the prices were outrageous."

While four of the five units in the mansion sold quickly, Parencorp found itself still having to sell one unit in the mansion and a free-standing renovated carriage house.

"I had a hard time convincing Gordon to spend $1,500 on a display ad," Diamond confides. "But we did. And a doctor came from the Back Bay holding the ad in his hand. We used 'The condo that isn't' to bill the carriage house, positioning it as a condo that isn't really a condo. We sold it almost immediately."

Parencorp also has managed to position itself as being environmentally sensitive. Again, the humble arrogance plays an important role. "We are very strong environmentalists," Diamond insists. "We just make sure people know what we do." "Environmental sensitivity" is indicative of Parencorp's commitment to excellence. In fact, it was awarded Brookline's Environmentalist of the Year Award in 1983 for placing a conservation restriction on land at the Sears Estate. Clever marketing alone doesn't spell success. It's also Parencorp's strong commitment to the highest quality product possible.

How do you make the market realize that while there are scads of competitors offering nearly the same product, yours is somehow different? Mabel and Henry may be compelled to buy a condo that was part of the historic Sears Estate, but not as compelled to buy a unit in a renovated dormitory.

Deciding How to Make Your Product Different

When Hal Gershman took over his father's business in 1976, Happy Harry's Bottle Shop had been operating in Grand Forks,

North Dakota, for 30 years. "I basically took the price and decided it was not going to be a major marketing tool because ours is a standardized product with price lists published by wholesalers, and price is the easiest thing to market."

So Gershman, who arrives late for our meeting in his office in the back of the Grand Forks store because the night before he had spearheaded an underdog effort to get a school renovation bond issue passed, decided instead to accentuate service and selection. "Our slogan became 'savings, service, and selection.'"

Deciding on a slogan doesn't constitute product differentiation. To be different, Happy Harry's had to be perceived as a place that truly offered savings, service, and selection.

"When the liquor industry decided to shift to metrics, it became confusing for the consumer," Gershman says. "We took some of the confusion out five or six years ago by becoming the first retail store in North Dakota of any type to unit price, posting the price per-ounce of all of our products. We even got letters from the government congratulating us.

"We were also the first and virtually the only store to bring in generic, no-frill liquor—everything from tequila to scotch—a total, no-frill label; just white and black with the words 'Scotch,' or 'Canadian,' or whatever."

Perceived as Different

Being perceived as "different" certainly hasn't hurt Happy Harry's. Over the past seven years, Gershman figures the firm has tripled in size. "We're the largest store in North Dakota, probably South Dakota and Montana as well. We probably have the largest volume from here west to Seattle."

In inventory, Happy Harry's has anywhere from $335,000 to $400,000 worth of wholesale liquor. Gershman is reluctant to say how sales are doing, but he will say, "You've got to do a hell of a volume to have that kind of inventory."

Gershman seems to thrive on his work, a trait he no doubt inherited from his late father, Happy Harry. "My father started downtown around 40 years ago. He had a restaurant down there. One night the chef left the steaks burning, and jumped off a bridge. My father said, 'If it drives a cook to commit suicide, it's no place for a Jewish boy.' So he opened the bottle shop."

Happy Harry's is also known as the place where you can get that nice little liqueur you always loved but never could find.

"We don't care if the liquor sells only four or five bottles a year. If it's one of those interesting items, that's part of our advertising. That's what makes our store interesting."

Interesting and different. "Our biggest gains, in fact, were during the 1981 recession," Gershman recalls. "Because we brought in generic labels and did unit pricing, people began to see us as a store considerate of the consumer trying to fight inflation. The growth from 1981 to 1984 was phenomenal."

Everything that Hal Gershman has done to make Happy Harry's a stand out from the crowd has been a conscious decision to differentiate his product. It's not that his product is better, it's that the difference he offers causes the customer to perceive Happy Harry's as better.

Deliberate Differentiation

"Everything we've done has been deliberate," Merrill Diamond of Parencorp states. Perhaps the most interesting product differentiation Diamond has had to-date has been with Parencorp's marketing of The Grand, a luxury condo complex in Brookline.

The Grand is a renovation of a hospital built in 1914. "It was originally called Greathill," Diamond says. "The last thing I wanted to stress was that you almost needed assistance going up the hill to the building. I also wanted a different notion that would eradicate the antiseptic feeling."

The answer was to use a 1930s art deco motif. "The view up there is incredible. It's as close as Brookline will ever come to having a Manhattan skyline view. Since I've been in Boston (since 1969), I've noticed a large cadre of people who think New York is better than Boston—theater, knishes, everything. Art deco is appropriate to catch that market."

Diamond created a history for The Grand. He differentiated it from everything else on the market in hopes of capturing a particular audience. "By going art deco, we're tossing out a whole section of the market," Diamond realizes. "Not empty-nesters or old Brahmins, but young professionals with money.

"Manhattan in the 1930s comes to Brookline in the 1980s is how we played it in the ads. We didn't focus on the building, but rather on the two major amenities, the view and a man and woman standing off to the side, which says it's not for empty-nesters or a college dormitory. Not swinging singles either, but certainly an enjoyable place to live."

Sometimes, as deliberate as he may be, Diamond latches onto a way to differentiate his dream products through on-site observation of the market's reaction to his product.

"At The Grand," he recalls fondly, "we had one penthouse unit. Somebody offered a lot of money for it, somewhere in the low five-hundred thousands. We decided then to take it off the market and reintroduce it as the 'Empire Suite.'

"We priced it at $1 million and planned a sophisticated television ad just on the Empire Suite. Interalia [an interior decorator in the same building as Parencorp] is decorating it. It'll raise the prestige of all the other unsold units, and at $300,000-plus, make them seem less expensive."

Diamond loves to sell, but at the core he's still an architect. "Gordon and I are both architects. He has much more of an architectural, quiet contemplative mind," Diamond admits. "My main concern is the effect a project will have on the marketplace and history. While Gordon may look at something for design, I look at the role in the marketplace. I love selling."

Selling by Reputation

Diamond says the company has actually sold units now based on reputation. "We up-played that we were architects. We not only use good materials, but we make sure everybody *knows* we use good materials. We not only insulate between the walls of condo units, we make sure people *know* we do.

"Because we've gone after quality, people will come to us. I like being clever as an architect. I can now carry that over into marketing. There were things that made Gordon and me want to be architects. We're still achieving that kind of satisfaction."

A Shinier Mousetrap

People come to places like Parencorp, Happy Harry's, and hundreds of other innovative businesses throughout the country, because they are perceived to offer something others don't. Peter Salisbury, president of the Boston-based Mercury Business Services, an overnight delivery service which takes advantage of volume discounts offered by Federal Express and passes savings plus added service onto its customers, defined product differentiation quite nicely. "Federal Express does those wonderful commercials," he says. "It's not that they're a better mousetrap, but shined-up a bit more, with maybe a better piece of cheese in it." All of these businesses have shined up their mousetrap and spent a little more on the cheese.

"Looking back on my life, I guess I always was a marketer, a salesman," says Diamond. "If it were 100 years ago, I'd be with a pushcart on Orchard Street."

MARKETING MESSAGES

Creativity is a magnet in the marketplace. By deliberately making their products stand out, entrepreneurs create a strong perception that their products give that something "extra."

Be a stand out in the crowd. Go for the unique. Let what's different about the product shine. Sometimes unique is translated by the market as "better."

The extra edge is product differentiation. When your company's name is mentioned let the market respond, "Oh yeah, that's the place you can get . . . ." Name recognition sells.

Chapter Six

Tailoring the Mundane Franchise: When You're Having More Than One

Jiffy-Lube is a chain of quick "pit-stop" oil change drive through franchises throughout the United States. It is the McDonalds of fluid maintenance, the Roy Rogers of auto service.

Dick Valentine owns the franchise rights to open Jiffy-Lubes within the Interstate 495 area of eastern Massachusetts. His first franchise is up and going in Braintree, just down the block from Quincy. His is a Jiffy-Lube with a twist.

Valentine is an avid race car driver. His Braintree Jiffy-Lube and all the promotion that's gone into it reflects his racing prowess.

"I'm driving from Thursday to Sunday," says Valentine, a stocky, solidly built balding man. Our interview took place at the Braintree offices of his MBA (Massachusetts Businessman's Association), Inc., a company Valentine started in 1969 to provide small to mid-size companies with all the insurance, financial services, data processing, and other business services they could possibly need, but couldn't afford to have, within their own company. "We're giving businesspeople a place to come to get all they need to carry on," Valentine explains.

"I'm an automotive person," he continues, explaining how he hit upon buying into the Jiffy-Lube concept. "I've got a lot of vehicles but couldn't get them serviced. I was exposed to Jiffy-Lube by people at Pennzoil Motor Oil Company."

Franchising into an Untapped Market

Valentine is selling quality: "We're making an investment in excellence. There are 120 million cars in America, 40 million vans and pickup trucks. Many millions of drivers need this kind of service. It's an untapped market—preventative fluid maintenance."

On the bookcase behind Valentine's desk, five cans of Pennzoil line one of the shelves. "I use Pennzoil exclusively in my cars. It's a tremendous motor oil." I expect that any minute Arnold Palmer will drive by on a tractor, confirming Valentine's endorsement. "With Jiffy-Lube, we're going to make a market share for Pennzoil in New England. Ours is a little company in comparison to Pennzoil. We respect the fact that they respect what we can do. I'll learn things from them. They may learn a little from me, who knows?"

Valentine recognized that as service stations stopped offering full service, a place like Jiffy-Lube could really take off. In 1978, there were 225,000 gas stations nationwide—66 percent were self-service, offering no fluid maintenance.

Valentine certainly knows his business, and he's quick to let you know about it, too. Notebooks, promotional write-ups, newsclips are all a part of his explanatory material. Throughout our meeting he'd get up and go to his door and say to his secretary, "Andy, can you put together . . . ?" Or, "Andy, do you have . . . ?"

"One of the keys to success here," says Valentine who wears Kelly green slacks, white shirt, green tie, and a leather jacket (an appropriately rugged look), "is having people follow up on things I do."

Tapping Extensive Market Expertise

Valentine has also been able to rely on the extensive experience he's had with marketing for MBA, particularly in the area of building up a data base of potential users. "I'm in marketing. I've data based every car owner in eastern Massachusetts," he boasts, creating a verb that a few short years ago wasn't even a noun, "and have put together my own mailing list."

From the results he's having, after investing $150,000 to get started in the Braintree Jiffy-Lube, it's obvious Valentine knows his market. "Right now in our first store we're outdoing national numbers, three to one," he says. "Average Jiffy-Lubes do 25-to-35 cars-a-day. Right now, we're averaging 60 cars-a-day. Within a matter of months, we'll be doing 90-to-100-a-day. Our goal within a year-and-a-half is to be doing 180 cars-a-day."

Custom-Tailoring the Franchise Stores

"We've basically used a lot of newsprint to promote our shop," Valentine tells me. "The 'Dick Valentine Racing Story.' It's basically a pit-stop operation, but nobody had yet taken a fast food approach to oil change."

Valentine is a practical man with a marketing know-how that comes from keeping up with what the market wants. By the time he was 16, he was working days at a slaughterhouse and driving a cab at night. In the summertime, he put in 14-to-15-hour days. In the mid-1960s, he enrolled in Suffolk University, continuing the cab driving job to put himself through.

"When I exited Suffolk," Valentine recalls, "I started Massachusetts Businessman's Association. I think my mother lent me

75 bucks to get started." In 1984, MBA managed about $78 million.

Hard work is implicit in Valentine's success formula. He also has a keen understanding of people. "I do a lot of deals in the trailer at races," says Valentine, who races in nine or ten races a year. "It's the only place where you can have people for three days in a fun, charged atmosphere. It's an aggressive, on-purpose sport. All in all, I feel marketing has to do with personal contact. Eye-to-eye, belly-to-belly."

Valentine uses the belly-to-belly approach by tailoring his Jiffy-Lube outlets to reflect his racing story.

"I'm a car nut. It's exciting," he declares as he scribbles a note to himself. He's an incessant scribbler, constantly jotting down ideas, reminders, numbers. "My wife finally got me a little pad with a light attached."

By diversifying into Jiffy-Lube and continuing on with MBA and his racing activities, Valentine can satisfy some of what he perceives to be the schizophrenic nature of the entrepreneur—satisfaction coming from dabbling in many different ventures, all with the distinctive stamp of Dick Valentine on them.

The Distinctive Stamp

Jiffy-Lube certainly has his stamp. It's a small brick building in Braintree, next door to a D'Angelos Sandwich Shop franchise and down the street from the Quintree Mall, so named for its close proximity to both Braintree and Quincy. When I drove up to Jiffy-Lube in my red 1978 Chevy Impala on a Saturday, there were about ten cars in line ahead of me for a Jiffy-Lube oil service, and three cars on line for a Jiffy Wash, which comes free with the complete $19.95 oil change. The free car wash, Valentine says, is something not every Jiffy-Lube offers.

You drive up to a sign, wait for the attendant, and fill out a checklist on a red clipboard. Saturday's the busiest day, so it takes about 25 minutes of waiting in line to get my car over the pit.

A Pennzoil model stock car is visible in the garage. In fact, there are Pennzoil promotions and products in quite a few conspicuous places. There's also a Coke machine in the garage. You can look straight through the garage when you're on line and see a whole stretch of fast food places on the same street. You can have your stomach and car served in one stretch. Franchise heaven.

I pull in at 1:35 over the pit, walk into the waiting area, where Charles, the attendant, announces, "That coffee's fresh. It hasn't been sitting there since this morning if anybody wants any." I do.

As I sip my coffee, I note that the walls of the waiting room are full of articles about Valentine and his racing laurels. Pictures of his cars are also abundant.

My oil's changed by 1:45. Charles tells me what they did. "That'll be $20.50." He instructs me to drive around to the car wash. "Someone will guide you through." I enter the car wash at 1:50. "Just drive in and the sign on the right will tell you what to do," another Jiffy attendant tells me. Indeed, it does. I'm out of there and back on the road by 1:55.

Tailoring the mundane franchise—that's what Valentine's success has been about. The key is taking something that others may be marketing and making it better. A black box is a black box, but my black box is better than yours.

Taking Something and Making It Better

The tailoring takes creativity. David Keeler and his partners, Donald and Daryl Levy, who are the owners of the six GOODS stores in the Boston area, certainly are creative. The story of tailoring their chain of stores has an unusual beginning.

"We started in Cambridge in 1975 as an eclectic department store carrying many different lines," David Keeler tells me as we're sipping coffee early on a Monday morning in Dave's, an ice cream shop on Newbury Street. GOODS' administrative offices are just down the street in this section of Boston's Back Bay. Keeler is a big man, probably 6′4″, and well over 200 pounds. He's soft-spoken and, in addition to a wry sense of humor, also appears to have a pleasant disposition.

"We had the store in Cambridge for three years. Then we opened at a second location at Faneuil Hall, where the traffic patterns are much different." Faneuil Hall is an historic landmark in Boston. The area has been renovated into a successful shopping area full of specialty shops and eateries.

The Same Store—With a Twist

Then, in 1980, the big idea hit. Rather than having one large eclectic department store in Cambridge, and a satellite store in Faneuil Hall, the GOODS people decided to recreate departments that existed in the original shop as stand-alone shops.

"In 1980 we sold the Cambridge store and changed the Faneuil Hall store," David recalls. GOODS now has six stores. The Faneuil Hall store opened in 1978 but was revamped in 1980. A GOODS lingerie store opened on Newbury Street in 1980. Another specialty gift shop opened on Newbury Street in 1982. A store specializing in designer goods opened in the Chestnut Hill Mall in Brookline in October 1984. Another gift shop and lingerie store opened in the spring of 1985 in the new Charles Square Mall in Cambridge's Harvard Square, not far from where the original GOODS had been.

"We look at what's available and try to see an opportunity for a proper audience," Keeler says, explaining how they decide on new locations. "Our stores get a certain tag. When people are looking for something different, they'll give us a look. Certain people will try to tag you. We've now established three if not four different looks. We also try to do in-store looks to associate people with our other stores."

Since the 'department as stand-alone store' concept took hold, GOODS has been doing very well. "Between operations we do sales somewhere between $2 and $3 million-a-year. Faneuil Hall accounts for about a third of that."

The reason that Faneuil Hall has worked so well for GOODS has a lot to do with the consistent traffic that flows through. "The Faneuil Hall store has always done well," Keeler says. "The marketplace doesn't work for any particular reason. It's a real potpourri. It's like what we do with our merchandise in a lot of ways. Some might be quirky, campy, queer, but it seems to fit together.

"Our market is fairly affluent, probably people who are going to appreciate our products. The average purchase at Faneuil Hall is probably lower because of the transience, but people there are not cost conscious. A lot of things at Faneuil Hall are based on the concept or situation. It's not a discount type of operation."

While some of the merchandise carried in the specialty gift shops overlaps, there are still distinctions between the stores.. "A lot of the merchandise is the same at Faneuil Hall and Newbury Street—giftwise and cardwise. But there's a more personalized service on Newbury Street. The Newbury Street store was one of the first stores to get those little folding robots from Japan. On Newbury Street it's not as crowded, so people can be waited on and given more background."

GOODS also tries to market its lines uniquely. "We've carried a couple of lingerie lines ever since we opened in Harvard Square," Keeler says. "We were the first to make it a fashion kind of thing rather than nuts and bolts. Now there's places like 'Victoria's Secret'."

A Distinctive Look

You can walk into any GOODS and, without even seeing any signs saying GOODS, you'll know you're in a GOODS. There's a feel about it. Something sort of quirky avant-garde. In the specialty gift shops, it's like being in a Roger Corman film—quality low-budget.

Keeler, who practiced law for five years before getting into retail, doesn't think there's any magic to the GOODS success. "There's a certain taste level to doing specialty retailing, but I think a fair amount of it is being practical," he says.

Like Valentine, who put his stamp on his Jiffy-Lube operation, the GOODS people have been able to put their stamp on each of their stores. As a result, rather than simply selling goods, they're selling GOODS.

Jiffy-Lube and GOODS don't want to be perceived as a series of carbon copy shops that offer exactly what the Jiffy-Lube or GOODS in the next town offers. By tailoring the chain, these shops have managed to retain a sense of distinctiveness in the marketplace. They might still be franchises, but their owners have used enough creative tailoring to let you know you're experiencing something different.

MARKETING MESSAGES

Take something others are doing and make it better. The true entrepreneur can take the carbon copy franchise concept and make it something special.

Find a distinctive stamp of identity. Fix it to your business and it instantly has an edge in the marketplace.

The eye-to-eye, belly-to-belly approach. Get next to your market, make contact, work hard to know your customers and understand their needs. It makes you a stand-out among the copy cats.

Chapter Seven

Creative Selling Propositions: Bringing Them Back for More

They say the heart of rock and roll is in Passaic. And from what I've seen I believe it.

Two doors down from the New Jersey Engineering and Supply Company in Passaic, is a rock and roll diner called "Eats-U-Want." Although it caters to a "rock and roll crowd," at lunchtime there are just as many gray suits sampling the eggplant parmigiana special as there are spike-studded leather-bedecked punk hairdos eating their standard fare of felafel.

With the help of sidekick Mr. ("Don't forget to mention") Foley, Mick Bello and Ayden Mir-Samesade (also known as "Ike," and other monikers, depending upon his mood) opened Eats-U-Want in August 1983, with an initial investment of about $20,000.

Mick, Ike, and I are sipping coffee as Mr. Foley works the lunch crowd at the counter. Behind him on a shelf is the torso of a mannequin dressed in a striped shirt and a chef's hat.

"We met in college," Mick tells me. Mick and Ike graduated from William Paterson College in 1980—Mick as an art major, Ike as a business major. "We probably did a lot more legwork and searched around more than other diner start-ups," Mick continues. "William Paterson sold us tables and commercial toasters for $5 each, and they're usually $200. We bought a cash register in upstate New York for $25, and a malted machine for $45. It took us about four months to set this place up."

Neither Mick nor Ike had food service experience, yet they were undaunted as they entered into a notoriously difficult business.

"When we were first starting out," Ike recalls, "our suppliers asked us if we had experience. We said no. They said you're crazy." So Mick and Ike, when asked, began to make up stories about their extensive diner career. "Yes, years in the business. Success after success," they'd say, no doubt receiving nodding approval from Mr. Foley. Ike is 26. Mick is 27. Mr. Foley's not talking.

When Eats-U-Want opened, the three of them who are "always there" certainly had their work cut out to draw in business. With limited resources they had to make every advertising penny count. In the beginning, they used a mailing list of 100 or so names from a rock club in Lyndhurst. They mailed an announcement of their opening to these names. "The first week was a madhouse," Mick recalls.

Using Creative Selling to Draw Crowds

Through a series of creative selling maneuvers, Eats-U-Want continues to draw the crowds. Early on, ads were run in a regional publication called the *Aquarian*. Written by Mr. Foley and illustrated with cutouts from old magazines purchased across the street at the Passaic Book Center, the ads announced that Eats-U-Want was going out of business, which it wasn't. But regulars and non-regulars flocked in as a result of the ad—either to help the eatery stay in business, or to witness its demise; no one's quite sure. Months later, new customers were still coming in saying, "I thought you were going out of business."

"We wanted a place that we would like to go to. We knew the places we liked," Mick says as Ike gets up to answer the phone. Mr. Foley pours coffee for a customer at the counter.

Eats now takes in somewhere between $5,000 and $6,000-a-month. Overhead's low—rent, $300-a-month; utilities, $400-a-month in the summer (when the air conditioner's going constantly), $200-a-month in the winter.

Ike returns. "There aren't too many places to go to in Jersey that are interesting," he says. "We offer a New York-like atmosphere in New Jersey."

Creating an Event

Creative selling, like Thursday night's pasta madness. All the pasta you can eat for only $2.49, with meatballs, just $2.99. Or the woman they paid to wear a sandwich board in front of the Capitol Theater in Passaic, while "The Stray Cats" rock band was playing, and hand out fliers offering "The Stray Cats Special," a burger, fries, and a Coke for a special low price.

On a larger scale, creative selling tactics have gotten Eats into the film and band business. Every Friday night, there's an alternating band and movie series. Tonight "The Willies" will be playing; next Friday, Eats will be showing "Children In Adult Jails."

Usually 70 to 80 people show up for a concert or film. The "Eats-Boys," as they like to be known, split the take at the door with the band or whomever they have selecting and showing the movies. The cover price is $3, and it's a B.Y.O.B. affair, which, according to Ike, "saves them lots of money on booze."

Events That Bring Back Business

More important than the take at the door has been the growth in business since beginning the series. "We started the film series and bands in September 1984," Mick tells me. "Business has grown because of the recognition. People come back." They come back not only for the bands and films, but also for daytime lunches and evening dinners when nothing special's going on during the week.

Ike chimes in, "With the bands and movies, total traffic has grown. Since our ad budget is small, we put no money up front for entertainment."

"Bands love the intimacy," Mick says.

Mr. Foley pours another cup of "jo."

Passaic, New Jersey, is a monster of a place to open up a new diner and expect to succeed. There are entire office buildings on the same street as Eats that are vacant, except for an occasional lone businessman who's been on Main Street for the last 50 years, and, by God, he'll stay there 'til they shut the place down.

But through creative selling techniques, the Eats Boys have made Eats-U-Want palatable to a tough audience. Creative selling techniques took the ordinary and turned it into something special. They took the fact that the upstairs of stores in the main area of town are not zoned for residential purposes and therefore limits nighttime drop-in business, and turned it into a positive by offering a Friday night band series where the chances of disturbing the peace became minimal.

Common-Sense Creativity

Creativity using common sense. Turning the mundane into something special. There are few who are better at it than "Mr. Florist" himself, Al Felly, owner of six Felly's Flower shops in Madison, Wisconsin.

"There are traditional flower days not observed anymore," Al says. "Like May Day." He pushes the button on his cassette recorder so I can listen to one of his radio ads.

"A tisket, a tasket, I'll deliver May Day baskets—for $1.95," Al Felly sings on the ads. Felly also takes advantage of Valentine's Day potential sales by advertising a Valentine's Day Rose Club.

"We advertise a dozen roses at $16.95. One now and 11 more throughout the year. Once we have the $16.95 to work with," Al says with his best salesman's grin, "we've got the guy in the store 11 more times during the year."

Felly makes the creative sell because he enjoys his business. "I like to sell flowers, but I like to sell *Felly's* flowers. That's what I'm in business for."

Inventing Events

But Felly doesn't rely solely on existing holidays. If the occasion warrants, he invents a holiday. Take his "Deer Hunter Special" as a case in point. "There are something like 400,000 deer hunters who take off each year," Felly says, explaining the market potential. "Everyone of these guys who takes off leaves a spouse at home who doesn't feel so good about it." Felly fiddles with the recorder and plays another radio ad: "I'll tell you how to get your deer. That's D-E-A-R. One dozen roses for $20 bucks." Corny, yes. But equally as creative, and most importantly, successful.

Going After the Biggest Potential Market

Felly's creative selling techniques come from simple marketing logic. He walks over to a flipchart, on which he's about to give a lesson.

"Let's say there are 1,000 deaths a year in Madison, with flowers costing $200 per funeral. That equals $200,000. There are 1,700 beds in Madison's hospitals. Let's say they're three-quarters full. That's 1,275 occupied beds. At one bouquet per patient per day at $10 dollars a bouquet, that comes to $12,750 per day. Let's say this occurs on 300 days during the year. That's a market potential of $3,825,000. As a marketing approach am I going to advertise funerals? Hey, I'm going to advertise towards hospital beds.

"Say there are 1,000 weddings in Madison. At $100 per wedding that's a $100,000 market potential. There are 7,500 anniversaries in June. At $20 a bouquet, that's a $150,000 potential in June alone for advertising an anniversary special. What am

I going to advertise weddings for? I advertise toward the greatest market potentials.

"Are you getting the idea that the market potentials haven't been tapped?" Felly asks. "The potential is amazing."

"We look for occurences where our product can be used," Felly continues. "There isn't a florist in our country who advertises for the day after Thanksgiving as a way of thanking the dinner preparer. This is a huge market."

Creating Reasons for Customers to Buy

But Felly doesn't just look for occurences to sell. He seeks to create a reason for the customers to buy.

"When we went into a recession," Felly says, recalling the early 1980s, "everybody advised us not to let people charge. Our sales started to flatten during the recession. We took a look at what we could offer for convenience and it was credit.

"The question was how to get people to pay their bills. We started to ask questions that could be filled out on the back of the charge slip. We started extending credit to everyone meeting the basic criteria based on the information on the charge slip. Sales went up. The average price per order went up."

Felly also started to send people a letter with their bills which included a recipe. Explaining that his rather rotund stature came from his love of food, Felly invited billpayers to send him a recipe with their payments. "We put the recipes through our kitchen and sent them out, one at a time, with the bills," Felly says. "We took all the recipes from over the years and came up with the *Felly Family Cookbook*, which we sell in the stores for $7.95.

"All of these ideas go into how we've come to have the largest sales per capita of all florists in all U.S. metropolitan areas."

The "Ego Sell"

One of the simpler, yet most creative selling techniques developed by Felly is the "ego sell."

"You rarely purchase an item," Felly explains. "You purchase a benefit. One of the benefits today is satisfaction of the ego. We price our roses individually. Rather than say $40 a dozen, we say $2.50 to $3.00 each. We don't want to damage the ego.

"We also label all of our products so it doesn't hurt the ego. Take Colangelas. By labeling it, the customer can immediately set up communication with the clerk. So a guy spends ten to twelve bucks on Colangelas.

"She says, 'What lovely flowers,' He says, 'What lovely Colangelas.'

"That night they have a dinner guest who the guy turns to and says, 'Say, how about those Colangelas?' The guest says, 'Sam, you're a smart son of a bitch.'

"You can bet Sam will come back to Felly's."

Marketing Messages

Creative selling brings the market back for more. Making each advertising penny count is the key, especially for the entrepreneur who is just getting off the ground.

Target the biggest potential market and create reasons to buy. Make it the event the market has been waiting for.

Use the "Ego Sell." Create proud, smart, clever customers. They spell repeat business.

Maxim Three

The Target-Practice Proverb

Aim for *Your* Market
and Shoot to Sell.
Pinpoint Your Market and
Never Let it Go.

You've got the product. You've added enough bells and whistles to at least cause the market to perceive that what you have to offer is better than what they can get elsewhere.

But if you're running a small to mid-size business, all too often the budget for capturing the market is not terribly large—certainly not large enough to waste on what you know is not the market for your product anyway. The answer is to target your market.

Targeting can take many forms. And with the introduction of new technology, the options for targeting a particular market segment have grown even larger. Witness the introduction of sophisticated direct mail marketing software and the impact it's had on a small wine shop in Brookline, Massachusetts. Or the advent of low-power television which, because it broadcasts in very limited market areas, can give the smaller business incredible opportunities to zero in on a particular market segment without incurring the kind of costs normal television advertising might run.

Technology isn't the only answer. Many of the more successful entrepreneurs profiled in the chapters that follow have succeeded because they picked a specific niche in the marketplace and have gone after that niche with a vengeance. They know their market—what it wants, what it'll buy, what it'll pay for particular products. They have a feel for the size and scope of the potential market universe. By gaining a thorough understanding of their targeted markets, they're often able to make subtle changes in product offerings that can please that target even more.

In some cases, savvy entrepreneurs are able to target a market within a market. If an expensive software product sells well to a market made up of upper management types, why not offer a less expensive version to middle management?

Targeting the market and giving it what it wants has been a key ingredient in the success of many small businesses. By targeting, these people are addressing a specific audience with specific needs. Often successful targeting means that the business must keep up with the latest trends and offer solutions to problems that the particular target market may face.

The companies that have targeted successfully continue to draw the business of a satisfied market. They have taken aim and, in many cases, hit a marketing bullseye.

Chapter Eight

Direct Mail List Management: And the Orders Pour In

London Wine Company has limited shelf space, limited floor space, and almost no parking area at its sole store in Brookline, Massachusetts. "This is a wonderful, safe area for elderly people. But those people don't drink very much," says owner Stephen Garber, who took over the family business a few years ago.

Garber realized that the kind of growth he was looking for—a one-year sales increase of 50 percent in 1985 to $1.5 million—wasn't going to come from increasing the foot traffic into the store, which is surrounded on each end of its Beacon Street block by a drug store.

Experimenting With Direct Mail

So Garber began to experiment with direct mail as a way to attract new customers and to coax established customers into bigger purchases. His first attempt was a monthly newsletter. Although the results were "less than overwhelming," they hinted at the potential that direct mail held for London Wine.

"We were heavily into shotgun-type mailings," recalls Garber. "We were blanketing areas. I had been considering going to a direct-response mailing house and doing some work with them."

Opting for Direct Mail Software

Instead Garber got some help from Selkirk Associates, Inc., a Boston-based software company that developed "The Selkirk Correspondent," a powerful direct mail management program designed to run on a personal computer. The $1,500 program, intended for business-to-business or big ticket retail direct mail, allowed London Wine to track each response and tailor its mailings to the tastes and needs of the individual recipients. The computer program vastly increased the efficiency of a notoriously ineffective marketing device, transforming it into a highly responsive, finely tuned instrument. The results have been dramatic.

In December 1983, a month after it began using Correspondent, London Wine's sales jumped 20 percent above the previous December's. By May 1984, Garber was calling it "almost the heart of our marketing operation." The company was racking up a 28 percent growth in sales for the year, and by the end of the first quarter of 1985, London Wine hit 50 percent.

"[Correspondent has] changed our company unbelievably," Garber says. After the first several months of using The Correspondent he admitted, "We're barely able to cope with the growth right now. We're all going bananas." After a year of using the software, he's a bit mellower. "We've matured. We're a lot calmer. We're less frantic about things." He does still complain about the lack of a quality computer printer to meet his needs.

The direct mail work has kept the company's computer, an IBM PC/XT, so busy that London Wine has had to buy a second one to get some other work done. "We were so busy doing Selkirk work that our accounting sometimes lagged behind," says Garber.

Direct Mail Software Possibilities

The emergence of such programs as Correspondent opens up broad possibilities for small companies that market to other businesses or to substantial retail customers. Such sophisticated software has been available for years to run on larger computers. But it is only recently that such complete direct mail management programs as Selkirk's Correspondent have begun to reach the personal computer market.

There is "a lot of junk out there," warns Craig Hucy, publisher of the newsletter, *Direct Response—The Digest of Direct Marketing*, and president of Infomat, Inc., a direct response advertising agency in Torrance, California. "There are about 30 software systems out there right now geared toward marketing, but there are not many that have an overall direct mail thrust to them. To be professional in today's marketplace, the emphasis needs to be on direct marketing."

In addition, there are plenty of list management programs and other less powerful types of software related to direct mail operations. But they cannot have the same sort of impact on an entire marketing plan.

Sweeping Impact of Software

At London Wine, the impact has been sweeping, changing not only the number of customers, but also the character of the customer base. "[Correspondent is] bringing us the kind of buyers we're looking for. It's bringing us people who want fine wine and are willing to buy it in significant quantity," Garber says. "We find some pretty wonderful wine at pretty wonderful prices. The business is becoming more and more finding the unusually wonderful values in wine. It is becoming more and more involved in selling what we want to sell, rather than what other people want us to sell. I only want to deal with a core of responsive wine users."

Target Specific Customers

"The idea of the product in terms of business-to-business direct mail is that we give a company the ability to, first of all, create very extensive information records on all their customers," explains Tony Merlo, one of the founders of Selkirk along with Allan Kennedy, co-author of the book *Corporate Cultures.* "But more importantly, the heart of the product is that we give them the ability to select specific customers with specific characteristics, based on all the information that they're keeping. They then can very efficiently be able to create a letter or something for mass communication that can be personalized to everybody in the group."

List Development

The first step in that process, as in any direct mail effort, is the development of a list. Rather than go the route of list brokers and list rentals, Garber decided it was more effective to develop his own list through what he calls his "crystal ball" method, a system that he is leery of describing in detail. "We took target groups in different areas and measured the response," recalls Garber. "Depending on what kind of response we were getting from the different people groups, we would saturate or forget them."

The First Mailing

After developing a list, London Wine mailed a general letter of introduction. The letter looked like anything but junk mail. It was typed on expensive stationery and mailed first class in a stamped envelope. "It looks like a personal letter, as if you would have your secretary type it," Garber says.

That first mailing consisted of several thousand letters, each accompanied by a business reply card and a brief overview of the store's offerings. At this point, notes Garber, "we didn't know what very many of their tastes were, so there wasn't a whole lot we could zero in on. The concept that we tried to promote throughout the first mailing was that of being a personal wine merchant."

Zeroing In on Responses

The zeroing in began after receiving the returned business reply cards on which respondents were asked to check off their interest in various types of wine. The mailing was followed by a telemarketing campaign, both to those who had responded and to those who hadn't. The response to the basic mailing was fairly low, so the telephone follow-up was essential to establish the data base of customers, which would serve as the starting point for all further marketing efforts.

After the telephone survey, London Wine developed a system for selecting customers from the data base according to their product preferences, and produced a letter for each customer based on his or her tastes.

"We had all different kinds of letters," Garber says. "All of those who responded to us by telephone or whatever got letters based on the preferences they had expressed. There can be two dozen or more versions of the letter."

Gaining Momentum

At first, Garber was disappointed with the response to his mailings.

"I wanted to grow 50 percent overnight in terms of sales," he says, recalling his initial optimism. "I had to stop and constantly keep asking myself what I was doing wrong. Why wasn't I getting the instant response? As I look back on it now, I did absolutely nothing wrong. I was just a little bit impatient. It all happened. It just took a little big longer. It's like trying to get a locomotive started. There's a period where it has to work pretty hard to start getting any momentum, but once it has a little momentum, it kind of goes on by itself. And that's what's happened now."

Garber claims that by using Correspondent to target an audience, he can, for example, market a $5 bottle of white Bordeaux to 300 prospects using direct mail, and sell 60 cases to individual or organization buyers.

Refining Marketing Goals and Skills

What's more, Correspondent has helped Garber refine his marketing goals and skills.

"The software isn't a management tool in the sense that it's a decision maker," cautions Tony Merlo. "You don't have a situation where it tells you that if this happens you should do this. It's an information builder, which allows a manager to go in and think about what to do with the information that is at his or her disposal."

Merlo attributes Garber's success to two factors: "There's the part of actually using the software, and there's the part of changing his business habits to take advantage of the software. The software doesn't make things happen," he insists. "You have to have a marketing structure, a marketing scheme in mind before the product becomes useful. It's our job as part of selling the software to go in there and force that kind of thinking."

Components of Correspondent Software

The Correspondent program is essentially an integrated data base and word processor. The data base consists of three different files, or types of capabilities. The first is a "people file" that allows users to profile in some detail who or what it is they are tracking. In the case of London Wine, Garber can profile a customer's name, whether it is an organization or a person, the address, and the customer's buying patterns and preferences.

The second part of the data base is an "activity file" that keeps a log of all the transactions that occur with each customer. So whenever London Wine sends a piece of direct mail, gets a phone order, or places a telephone call, the transaction is recorded.

An "event file" is the third part of the data base. This serves as a scheduling device for things that should happen in the future. If London Wine gets a phone call today placing an order for two weeks from now, it cannot only record the order in the activity file, but also schedule in the event file that in two weeks it will have to make the delivery. The event file can be called up for a given week, and all the events that should take place during that week will be displayed, resulting in an effective "tickler file."

The word processing of Correspondent allows the user to compose documents from scratch or to store documents that can be retrieved at a later date. Because Correspondent's word processing and data base systems are integrated, it is relatively easy to call up and print out desired labels of names with specific characteristics from the data base, as well as create a direct mail campaign complete with a series of follow-up letters that can be stored in the system. The preferences of individual customers can be called up and used to personalize letters that are composed on the word processing portion of the software. And reports on how a particular mailing performed are easily produced.

Correspondent operates on the IBM PC, IBM PC/XT, or any IBM-compatible hardware with 256 kilobytes of random-access memory, a 10-megabyte hard disk, a display monitor, and a letter-quality printer. It sells for $1,500 for the barebones diskette with instruction manual, or $4,000 for customized software with some applications consultation, plus $400-a-day for additional Selkirk consultation.

The information-building and organizational capabilities of Correspondent have been a godsend for Garber in managing the increase in his business.

"There's about 80 things going on at the same time," he says. "We try to do some prospecting every month, say a few hundred letters, followed up by telephone calls within a coule of weeks after the letters go out. There's also a certain amount of direct telemarketing, even without letters, with positive response stuck in the data base. Then there are the mailings to the entire list of people who are active in the program. We try to get a piece out every four to six weeks. A good deal of our time is being drained in filling all the orders coming in."

So far, London Wine has limited the use of Correspondent to its retail store, which had 1984 sales of almost $1 million. While Correspondent was not commercially available until January 1984, the company has been using it since November 1983 as a part of Selkirk's test program. London Wine will use the software in 1985 for its wholesale arm, Eastern Wine Cellars, Inc., which Garber estimates will do more than $1.2 million in sales in 1985, its first full year of operation. "It will allow our wholesale salespeople to track business and not lose sight of that business," says Garber.

Correspondent is not the only software on the market that is capable of doing a complete business-to-business direct-mail campaign, however. Binary Systems Inc., of Newton, Massachusetts, developed a software package called "Market Master," which is similar to Correspondent in some capabilities. For a while, however, the software, called "Executive List Management," was available for use only on the Canon computers for which Binary is the New England manufacturer's representative. An IBM version of Binary's Market Master is now being marketed through N-Sure Systems Inc., in Monroe, Louisiana, which markets IBM PCs with specially tailored software to insurance brokers, agents, and companies. By the time Garber had his system up and running, N-Sure had sold about 15 Market Master packages at $895 a shot; but, to N-Sure's knowledge, none of the purchasers had the system up and running at that time.

Selkirk's customers seem pleased with the program. Softbridge Microsystems Corp., for example, a software development firm in Cambridge, Massachusetts, which is developing software for financial planners, purchased Correspondent software not only for its direct mail capabilities, but also to use in prospecting for customers and conducting market research. Cathy Cassia, who works in Softbridge's marketing department, has been using Correspondent for two months. She describes it as an "unbelievably easy system."

"I don't even want to discuss the other marketing software I used," says Cassia. "It was here when I got here and was probably much less expensive. But it was deadly. Correspondent just spells it all out."

MARKETING MESSAGES

Direct mail software can build a responsive customer base. A growing number of good software packages and the diminishing costs of personal computers spell enormous opportunities for the entrepreneur.

Use software as an information provider. The right software lets you track market response and customize mailings to individual needs.

Build slowly. Gain momentum. Direct mail is the entrepreneur's ticket to the Age of Technology. Never forget that patience, persistence, and experimentation are vital to success in all aspects of marketing.

Chapter Nine

Zeroing In with Low Power TV and Tunnel Radio

LOW POWER TELEVISION

Rick Hutcheson is a tall, lean, serious-minded businessman, who, through the low power television stations owned by his Low Power Television Development Corporation (LPTDC), may offer a solution for the small business that wants to use television to target a specific audience.

"The bottom line is that it's television," Hutcheson tells me in his Vienna, Virginia, office. Hutcheson was staff secretary for President Carter, and his office holds artifacts from his stint with that administration—framed snapshots, collected and bound presidential papers, and an Andy Warhol print of Carter which is signed by the former president.

Low power television is indeed television, but as its name implies, it is television with greatly limited power. "They're 1,000 watt, 1-kilowatt stations," Hutcheson explains, "which reach a 10- to 35-mile radius. A conventional station is 500 kilowatts and typically reaches up to 75 miles. Our entire investment for one station is $500,000. That's the cost of a conventional station's transmitter alone."

LPDTC now owns and operates three stations. The first was TV51 in LaSalle, Illinois. The second, TV42 in Ottumwa, Iowa; and the third, TV38 in Jackson, Tennessee.

"We're projecting $10,000 in ad sales a month for the first year," says Hutcheson. "Our ultimate goal is to have 30 stations, which would put us in the 75- to 100-million household range. Then we could attract national advertising."

Until that time, low power television is great for the little guy to get on the airwaves. "We hit roughly 40,000- to-50,000 people per-station," says Randy Swingle, formerly general manager in LaSalle, but now based in Vienna as vice president for all of LPTDC. "Our cost of ads is similar to radio stations in the area. Plus, we offer the obvious benefits of the video side of ads. The ads can range as low as $8 and as high as $35 for 30 seconds. They average $12-to-$14 to run for 30 seconds. In LaSalle, most people realized we were giving them the opportunity to advertise on television at the same cost level as radio or the newspaper." The prices do not include production, which the low power stations will also provide for a fee.

Testing Narrow Markets

Hutcheson also points out the incredible potential low power television offers once it gets running on a national basis. "Once we get where we're able to do ratings on a national basis, we'll be able to test products at an incredibly low cost compared to nationally.

"Say you want to get out the vote and decide to target the black audience. You can use radio, but with low power television you can advertise microcommunity by microcommunity. It could revolutionize television advertising. Cable never really got into the advertising business like low power television promises to."

In the conference room of the Vienna offices where videotape equipment is set up I ask Swingle about his experiences in

LaSalle. It soon becomes clear that talking about low power television revs his enthusiasm.

"Twice in Illinois we conducted some audience research which showed we reached four out of five households in the area. We finished fifth out of 30 possible stations these people could watch. The three networks, plus WGN out of Chicago, were the only ones ahead of us. We finished ahead of the more popular cable networks. After only a year we were able to take a significant share of the audience there."

Swingle sets up the videocassette player, and plays a taped tour of the LaSalle station. Advertisers include Peru Savings and Loan, Morrari's Restaurant, Barto Auto Repair Service, Judith R woman's shop, among others. In addition to about three hours of local daily programming, LPTDC runs a lot of old movies and some old television series which include, "Peter Gunn," "Peyton Place," and "Dark Shadows."

"A single episode of 'Magnum PI' might cost $50,000 to run," Hutcheson says as he enters the room. "It might cost us $5 to run an episode of 'Peter Gunn' or a movie might cost $19."

LPTV Auction—Capturing More Ad Dollars

One of the more innovative moves to attract advertisers which Swingle used after about 10 months on the air in LaSalle was a phenomenon known as "TV Auction."

"I kind of stole this from radio," Swingle explains as he presses fast forward on the VCR, trying to find clips of the auction. "We went to advertisers we couldn't get on the air or who thought they couldn't afford us, and got them to give us products they couldn't sell. We left the products in their stores and announced them ahead of time so people could go look at them.

"We then aired live, taking bids. We'd keep the money from the sale, and give the retailer a credit for advertising air time worth the same amount. We created $20,000-to-$25,000 worth of revenue from sources we never had before. We started airing at 5:20 p.m., after business hours. We'd promote a week ahead of time. We found that audience participation for the show was phenomenal.

"You want to be in operation six-to-nine months before you try it," Swingle warns, "because you want to be able to identify advertisers you aren't likely to get."

LPTDC has only been on in LaSalle since October of 1983, so the verdict is still out on how successful a vehicle TV51 is for advertisers. But advertisers keep going back to it, even if they're not always sure it's working like it should.

Spotlighting Out-of-the-Way Business

Judith Reitgraf, who owns her own boutique, "Judith R," in Peru, Illinois, continues to advertise on TV51. "I'm not in the downtown area and I'm not in the mall," Reitgraf explains. "I advertised with them during the Christmas holidays."

For under $500, Judith R advertised on a special style show that was being packaged in conjunction with Total Image, a fitness/makeup salon. "For a package of nine fashions which ran 36 times, it cost us $450 on the style show," she says.

Almost six months later, Judith still wasn't sure how it worked, but she was going with them again. "I am running another ad on television that cost $288—just to give it a chance and see what the reaction is."

Better Response Than Print Ads

Niles Barto, who, with his son Buck, owns Barto Repair Service on Airport Road in LaSalle, told me, "We're away from the business district as far as auto repair is concerned. So we ran a 30-second film ad this summer. The newspaper ad we had run didn't seem to do us any good. We got more from the TV51 ad.

"We just jotted some ideas down. TV51 set the whole thing up. They told us to watch it and tell them whether we liked it. It ran four months during the summer. They did a real satisfactory job on it. Real satisfactory."

The Bartos spent a little more than $900 for their ad, a price which included production. The ad ran four nights a week, one time a night, for four months. "They'd run it twice for us sometimes at the same price," says the senior Barto, a mechanic for 14 years, eight of them for Chevrolet, before he trained his 24-year-old son and opened up Barto Repair Service.

"The newspaper had cost us around $37 for each ad," Barto says. "We probably put around $500 worth of ads in the paper. People pick up the newspaper and skip through it. They sit and watch television and see the ads—not all of them, of course, don't get me wrong."

TUNNEL RADIO

Using a medium that goes into a specific, isolated marketplace is an ideal way to target a market. Because the market reach is small, there's the added advantage that the cost is usually smaller, too. Low power television gives smaller businesses in the LaSalle area a chance to share the glamour of television without sharing an equal burden of the cost.

Tunnel Radio in Boston presents an even more targeted market—one tunnel in downtown Boston. Every day, almost 191,000 vehicles pass through the 2,385-foot, six-lane South Station (Dewey Square) Tunnel in Boston. Since June of 1982, the AM reception on the radio in each of those cars has shifted from static to continuous broadcast of Tunnel Radio, a broadcast operation owned by Rador Inc., a 56-year-old family billboard advertising company based in Springfield, Massachusetts.

Highway Communication

From his office on Lincoln Street, which overlooks his tunnel operation, Alan Radding, one of Tunnel Radio's principals, tells me, "There's a connection to the billboard business. Tunnel Radio is highway communication."

For $12 per 30-second ad, an advertiser can book time on Tunnel Radio. "Tunnel Radio trespasses on the major Boston media and . . . can give a smaller business the opportunity to cut into a major media for a much reduced price," says Radding.

"Funny you asked me about Tunnel Radio," Erik Scott, president of his family's 75-year-old Atlantic Marine Supply store, which did between $1.2 and $1.6 million in sales in 1984, laughed. "I wasn't even going to use it at first. I really didn't believe in Tunnel Radio. I thought it was quite kooky."

Marginal Cost, High Response

Kooky it may have been, but after advertising mobile car radios for just one week, Scott got 100 responses, 20 of which turned into purchases of their "Cellular One" car phone, which retailed at the time for $1,995. "I didn't get that type of response from the *Globe* or the *Herald*, Scott admits. "We were running the ad weekly every hour for under 30 seconds. It was costing us $300-to-$400-a-week, which is marginal compared to what we're selling."

But Scott isn't sold on using Tunnel Radio. Once it caught on with other advertisers, his ads weren't repeated as often, and he's stopped using it. "It was wonderful at the beginning. At the end we got dribs and drabs. But Tunnel Radio is absolutely cheap. The *Globe* is very expensive—one-eighth of a page costs $2,500-to-$3,500. It's outrageous, but the best means I have," says Scott, in spite of the fact that Tunnel Radio out-pulled the *Globe* for a time.

"I guess it was just saturation," Scott says when he tries to figure out a reason for the drop in responses.

Other advertisers don't share a bit of his skepticism. Phil Ressler, advertising director for Worldwide Electronics, a retail electronics discount house in Braintree, which sells around $3.5 million worth of stereos, radios, televisions, and other electronics items a year, is sold on Tunnel Radio.

"We're buying the 25-to-54 year-old marketplace, predominantly men," Ressler told me. "We have a suburban location, so we're interested in people with cars, a job, and money to spend. Tunnel Radio seemed to be an inexpensive way to roughly target our audience. That audience clearly has cars and jobs.

"We view Tunnel Radio as a billboard substitute," Ressler continues, indicating that he's truly been sold on the Tunnel Radio pitch. "It's much cheaper than a billboard on the Southeast Expressway would be. I never spend more than $2,000 [a month] on it, sometimes as little as $800.

"Our location is good for our wholesale end (about $6.5 million-a-year in sales), but not retail. There's a perception in the Boston market that Braintree is harder to get to than it is. Tunnel Radio was an inexpensive way to get my name in their ears. It's an excellent reinforcer for our other ads on the radio."

"Guerrilla Advertising"

Worldwide has also used Tunnel Radio for a "guerrilla advertising" campaign which Ressler launched against one of its chief Boston-area competitors, Manufacturer's Marketplace. "They were buying spots two to three times our frequency and surrounding me," Ressler recalls. "I tried to use hit-and-run tactics against them—guerrilla advertising. Tunnel Radio was perfect for that."

From the last quarter of 1983 to the last quarter of 1984, Worldwide Electronics experienced, according to Ressler, "well over 100 percent growth." He doesn't hesitate to credit a good portion of that growth to Tunnel Radio.

How Tunnel Radio Works

Tunnel Radio was born when Rador cut a deal with the State of Massachusetts back in December 1981 to "rent" the tunnel-airwaves. The company pays the state $500-a-month and 10 percent of any income over $300,000. Currently, according to Radding, revenues from ad sales are "a few hundred thousand," still shy of the $300,000 mark.

Radding says Rador has a 10-year lease with a 5-year renewable option. Because Tunnel Radio is owned by a privately held company, Radding believes that the major loss suffered in 1983 and the small loss suffered in 1984 will not shut down the station. He's optimistic that 1985 will be the first profitable year. "The mission of the company is to provide secure, interesting jobs and not lose money in the process. We will not," continues Radding, "jeopardize the future of other jobs in the billboard business to maintain a loser."

All indications are that Tunnel Radio will be around for a while. The advertiser renewal rate is reportedly doing very well, somewhere in the area of 70-to-75 percent. Advertisers tend to spend between $600-to-$2,000 on programming on a weekly and monthly basis. Tunnel Radio only charges the advertisers for peak times of traffic. During the middle of the night, for instance, spots will be repeated free of charge.

Tunnel Radio can never turn into a 24-hour advertisement station. The state requires that half of the air time be used for public service announcements. They also have a cut-in microphone for use in traffic emergency warnings.

Tunnel Radio is also receiving some competition. Beginning in late January 1985, Commuter Communications began broadcasting in the Callahan and Sumner Tunnels which lead to and from Boston and Logan Airport. While the concept is similar, the mechanics are quite different.

On all nine AM stations, the Commuter Communications signal will be received for the first 1,500 feet, in which it can ask the listener to turn to a fixed Commuter Communications AM band. If the driver doesn't, the regular programming will resume. Tunnel Radio, on the other hand, will capture whatever AM station you're listening to and keep it for the duration of your drive through the South Station Tunnel.

It's the automatic capturing of the AM airwaves that makes Tunnel Radio such an attractive mechanism with which to target a market. "Many people don't have the slightest idea that the programming's changed once they go into the tunnel," says Worldwide's Ressler. "Whenever I would run something on WRKO or WEEI, it was an excellent reinforcer. We got more response when we added Tunnel Radio to other radio advertisements.

"Now I wouldn't run major radio advertising without Tunnel Radio."

MARKETING MESSAGES

Think "microcommunities." For targeting specific markets, low power television and Tunnel Radio offer entrepreneurs innovative, low-cost ways to target specific markets.

Less reach, less cost. Tunnel Radio gives small advertisers a chance to "trespass" on major city media. Tunnel Radio and low power television are inexpensive reinforcements to any ad campaign.

Don't be put off by "alternative media." The entrepreneur on the look-out for the latest innovations in marketing might consider these a real boon to a limited advertising budget.

Chapter Ten

Market Niches: The Universe is Their Oyster

"What you have with *Cobblestone* is a publication for kids, 8-to-14, who are readers. There's no question that *Cobblestone* is aimed at the better reader," Lyell C. "Ted" Dawes, publisher and president of Cobblestone Publishing, says as we sit in his Peterborough, New Hampshire, office. *Cobblestone* was started as an educational but still entertaining children's history magazine as a clear attempt to target a specific, albeit large, market niche—reading children.

Marketing a product to a specific market niche is one way of having a good idea of how many potential buyers are out there for your product, a firm sense of your universe. It would be naive to assume that identifying a market niche spells success. Categories can be identified and labeled as needing this or that, but if the category is too limiting, there's little chance the product would achieve much success. Even if every person interested in butterfly entrails subscribed to a four-color glossy magazine on the topic, to use an example given to me by Carl Gnam, one of the cofounders of *Military History* magazine, the likelihood of making a profit on such a publication is minimal. The universe is too small.

Not so with all publications that target a specific market niche and go after it with a publication appropriate in scope, size, and cost to capture that market profitably. "It's not always a question of whether you can achieve goals," Ted Dawes reminds me, "but whether you can achieve profits."

Publications like *Cobblestone*, *Military History*, the books published by Bankers Publishing Company, and even a small cheaply printed monthly newsletter like *Gore Gazette*, which caters to fans of camp exploitation (formerly known as horror) films, can succeed because they have an idea who makes up their universe. By keeping that universe in mind, in terms of size and concerns, these specialized publications can market to a specific niche, and ideally not lose any money in the process.

THE ROAD TO *COBBLESTONE*

The idea comes first.

"I was teaching at the time and there wasn't enough material for the middle grades," says Hope Pettegrew, one of *Cobblestone's* founders, who now serves as its business manager. In the fall of 1978, Fran Nankin, the other founder who is no longer with the magazine, and Pettegrew began to meet once a week to discuss the possibility of starting a publication. "We weren't even sure of the format at the beginning," Pettegrew recalls. "We thought about a newsletter at first, but didn't want to compete with *Weekly Reader*.

"Fran Nankin became the editor. She wrote the entire first two issues. I became the publisher. The first mailing went out in October 1979 and we promised the first issue by January 1980. We mailed out 100,000 marketing pieces, and got a 2.5 percent to a 'soft offer.'" Pettegrew explains that a soft offer is when a direct mail offer doesn't require money up front, but rather gives the potential subscriber a "bill me later" option. While the return rates are typically higher with a soft offer, it is sometimes misleading, because the payment rate of the bill me option is not always as high as the marketer would like. A "hard offer" asks for the money up front, no questions at all about later payment.

Cobblestone got its 2.5 percent response and found 2,500 subscribers at $12-a-year. Those first subscribers represented readers from every state in the United States.

"We mailed to teachers magazines, other kids magazines, special interest magazines for adults," Pettegrew recalls. "The very best list was the FAO Schwartz toy store catalog list, which pulled 4 percent. We did our next mailing in January or February of 1980 to a lot more names. I think we pulled a 3.8 percent response on that one."

Cutting Costs to Increase Profits

Cobblestone boasted a 20,000 circulation by the following June, Pettegrew says. "We had incredible public relations and continued growing, but the soft offer kind of hurt us. We didn't have any advertising and we were relying entirely on subscription sales for revenue. We quite quickly raised subscription rates, dropped the two colors we were using on the inside of the magazine, and lowered the weight of the cover."

By the middle of 1982, *Cobblestone* had a 35,000 circulation. But in the fall of 1981, Pettegrew recognized that *Cobblestone* needed input from a professional source.

"I realized the job was more than I wanted to do for 16 hours every day. I had been a first grade school teacher. It got to the point where it was obvious we needed help. We hired Ted Dawes in the fall of 1981 as a consultant who'd come up once a month and spend three days with me."

By March 1982, Dawes was hired to run the magazine as full-time publisher.

Dawes is an affable man—a talker, really more a spinner of yarns. I can't help but think as we sit in his office on Grove Street in Peterborough, the "town" of Thornton Wilder's *Our Town*, that he'd make an excellent Down East radio talk show host. It's a surprise to learn that he's not a native New Englander. Dawes was born in Baltimore and spent most of his working life in New York and California. Dressed in tweedy, dark gray flannel pants, a blue Oxford cloth button-down shirt, and a plaid tie, Dawes would just as easily appear at home coming up from the big city to run the local newspaper, like Cary Grant in *Penny Serenade*.

"I'm a great believer in a mild degree of fate in what you do—a combination of fate and will. The toughest thing is the fate. You don't always know when the money's going to come through. I really believe our product is good," Dawes says.

Dawes was charged with making *Cobblestone*, which currently has 41,000 subscribers, a profitable venture. "What happened that first year was grim. It was a combination of dramatic cost cutting, renegotiating some agreements with printers and other vendors. The last two years, 1983 and 1984, have been profitable. One of the secrets in our business is to keep overhead down. In publishing I try to shoot for sales per-employee of $100,000. With a staff of ten, we're nowhere near that now."

Recognizing Niche Problems

"You've got two basic problems with children's subscription publishing," Dawes says. "You just get them hooked and they outgrow it, and there's no advertising. When I didn't have any ad revenue, which in subscription publishing is typically the profit with circulation breaking even, I had to decide if there was any way to make this thing go. The answer seemed to be to get into the school market because they won't outgrow it. You build credibility with the schools and then sell them other things.

"I've been pushing hard to get *Cobblestone* used as a solid classroom tool, not just in the library," says Dawes, who explains that the circulation is split fairly evenly between schools and individual buyers. "We keep an index of back issues and say to schools, 'Buy all 65 and get an index and let the kids interact with these things. You'll get a better thing than a text.'"

New Packaging Can Broaden Appeal

Packaging back issues has been a real boon to *Cobblestone*'s sales. "Ted has really pushed back issues," Hope Pettegrew tells me. "He has created what he calls 'The *Cobblestone* Library,' which he sells as a set for the year in a box with an index. He has really done an incredible job with that kind of marketing strategy. A lot of schools will buy many copies of that same issue. Now we've developed a teacher's guide which again will help with back issue sales."

But the school market is not without its problems, Dawes admits.

"What I'm most worried about is the crunch in the schools since about half of our income comes from them," he says. "We are heavily dependent on schools. In the past, school spending for materials came to just less than 1 percent of total spending for schools. Seventy percent of the spending is for people. If you could get more money to teachers with a leaner administration, you'd get a better education. Of that 1 percent on materials, probably 85 percent is now going for textbooks. And what's happened is that they've been written down, down, down. Books for high school are now written on the fourth-grade level.

"I believe in being the highest-priced person and being able to prove your quality," Dawes confesses. "Almost all of our subscriptions, around 90 percent, are now paid up front. We're the highest-priced children's magazine along with *Cricket.* I believe in selling what you have and standing behind it."

Dawes notes that *Cobblestone* currently has a circulation of around 41,000, "which I tend to try to keep fairly steady. I think the optimal size is probably between 60,000 and 90,000. The average order is $30. We're selling a lot more than just the $18.50 subscription."

He says the renewal rate is high in the schools; if they like it, they're going to stay with it.

Profit Potential

"There is a profit potential in it. You've got to work awfully hard to do it, keep overhead down, but keep the quality of the product up, too."

While Dawes can talk ad infinitum about profit potentials and cost cutting, it's clear that he's also convinced that his publication serves a worthwhile purpose. "We think we're providing a unique tool in education and entertainment in the home," he says.

In addition to *Cobblestone*, the company now publishes two other magazines—*Calliope*, which focuses on the classics and is geared to a primary market, and *Faces*, which was acquired through the Museum of Natural History in New York in 1984, and has an anthropological bent. Both publications, acquired within the past two years by Cobblestone Publishing, are currently still early in their circulation growth.

When Dawes is asked if he is responsible for turning *Cobblestone* into a profitable operation, he comments: "Jack Kennedy had a great saying that I think he took from history—'Victory has a thousand fathers, defeat has only one.'"

One of the reasons *Cobblestone* needed to bring a person like Ted Dawes in to help steer it through was, at least Hope Pettegrew feels, because the original capitalization had been lower than necessary. The company raised $110,000 from investors in the beginning which was probably too little.

BATTLING FOR THE NICHE

Adam Landis and Carl Gnam, however, would have given their eye teeth for even a small portion of that nestegg when they were beginning Empire Press in 1983 in Herndon, Virginia. Empire Press was started on a combined investment of $300 from the company's cofounders, 27-year-old publisher Landis, and 31-year-old editorial director Gnam. Gnam and Landis had worked in advertising production, so they had an idea how to do things cheaply. Their story is also a story of going after a particular market niche.

They began their first publication in February 1983, a quarterly magazine called *Living History*, aimed at people involved in historic reenactments.

"Living history is a subject I'm familiar with, and I knew there was no magazine addressing that market," Gnam explains during an interview in Empire Press' two-room office suite rented for $325-a-month in Herndon, about 10 miles outside of Washington, D.C.

Working on a Shoestring Budget

"We got unit mailing lists at first," recalls Landis, who oozes enthusiasm whenever he discusses the success Empire's had, "a lot of clubs and things for free. The first mailing for *Living History* was an inexpensive 11 × 17-inch two-color mailer. First we sent out 100 mailers at a time and got some money back. For the first three issues of *Living History* we did our own fulfillment."

Gnam, the calmer member of the duo, adds: "We printed up 600 or 1,000 of the promotion pieces and went to a battle reenactment and started handing it out. The next weekend we had 300 subscriptions. That's when we started asking reenactment groups to send us their membership lists.

"We did the *Living History* promotional and got 1,000-to-1,500 subscribers for the first issue. Everybody loved that first issue," boasts Gnam.

Landis and Gnam continued to put the money they were making on subscriptions back into the company to pay for production and marketing costs. *Living History*'s circulation grew to around 25,000 by the end of 1984, garnering advertising income between $6,000 and $7,000 an issue.

Using Profits for More Ambitious Projects

By the end of 1983, Empire Press had grossed only about $30,000, but it was enough to get the ball rolling on a more ambitious project, the bimonthly *Military History.* The start-up investment was certainly more than the original $300 that launched *Living History. Military History* is targeted at a broader market niche than *Living History*—the military enthusiast.

"We wanted to do a high quality magazine to showcase our talents," says Gnam. "I had worked at an ad agency and as art director for *FBI Magazine.* I learned how to deal with printers. I learned in a simplistic way the problems we might face. *Living History* had already given us a good credit rating with printers, which was one of our main goals."

"Initially we paid for three space ads," says Landis, who grabs a candy bar from a box of junk food on one of the desks in the office. "After we had enough orders to pay for postage, we did direct mail. We did a small test of 500 of our own names and got a 60 percent response in May 1984. In June, we did a 20,000 test of four different lists. We got a 19 percent return of orders with money. Breakeven was a 3.5 percent return. In August we did another mailing of 150,000 and pulled a 6.3 percent response."

Building an Advertising Base

By the middle of 1985, *Military History* boasted a circulation of more than 125,000, 45 percent subscription sales, 55 percent newsstand. "We try to use newsstand sales and advertising to pay for the production of the magazine," says Landis. "But it takes around one-and-a-half-to-two years for a magazine to build up a good advertising base. Our advertising now brings in about $15,000 an issue, while our print bill runs $28,000-to-$42,000 an issue. Fulfillment and mailing costs run around $200,000-a-year for about 88,000-to-90,000 subscribers. You have to pay the post office and the fulfillment house in cash. That's a pretty heavy bill for us to be meeting every other month. If we're up to 100,000 paid subscribers, we're talking renewal money of $750,000. That's $250,000 for billing, postage, and other expenses, and $500,000 profit."

"We haven't quite figured out what our universe is," says Gnam, who admits it's "a term we learned when we started doing direct mail. It's larger than we thought."

Adds Landis, "We think it's around 250,000 paid."

"If we knew everything we know now when we first started," confesses Gnam, "we might have been too frightened to do it the way we did it."

One of the harder things Gnam and Landis had to face when launching *Military History* was fighting the image of being a *Soldier of Fortune*-type magazine. They perceive their image more along the lines of sophisticated four-color history publications. They get all of their art for free from various military service branches. "It's government owned and free to use," says Gnam. "They love to see us down there because their stuff doesn't get printed very much."

Gaining Acceptance Is Tough

It hasn't been easy going gaining acceptance in the marketplace. Gnam and Landis wanted to get funding early on, but were always informed that it wasn't available. When *Military History* was first coming out, Landis' trip to New York City to find a newsstand distributor met with equally distressing results. "They just snubbed us," he recalls.

Ed Handi, president of Capital Distributing Company in Derby, Connecticut, which distributes around 130 titles, including magazines like *Gung Ho*, decided he'd take on *Military History*. "We sold 40 percent of the issues the first time out. We became Capitol Distributing's flagship," boasts Landis.

Gnam adds, "Of course, the distributor, wholesaler, and retailer all get a cut of the cover price. We get a check every 30 days. They like the quality. We like the service they're giving us." The distributor takes approximately 3 percent of the cover price, while Empire ends up with about 54 percent when all cuts are made.

When he recalls the original snubbing by distributors, Gnam says, "Here was a fantastic idea staring them in the face. So the heck with them."

Capitalizing on the Niche

With the success of *Military History*, Empire Press continues to grow and branch out. Like *Cobblestone*, back issue sales have been an unexpected source of income. Empire Press also marketed a 10-tape series of videocassette battle tapes, which clears $25-per-tape.

Gnam and Landis have targeted a market niche and capitalized on it. "A year ago we didn't even have $2,000 in the bank," says Landis. "Now we just bought a townhouse that Empire Press is going to rent out as an investment. We have $100,000 in liquid cash assets. We're so current on bills, they go out the same day we get them. We're paying in advance on printing bills and getting a 5 percent discount."

Observes Gnam, glibly, "We run our business differently from most publishers; consequently, we have a hard time relating to them. Someone described us as entrepreneurs, not publishers. *GEO* magazine just went out of business. They were losing

$500,000-a-month. That's ridiculous. They should have given it to us and we would have made a profit on it."

"We're not bright guys here," Landis effuses, Clark Bar in hand. "We're just simple, hard-working slobs with a lot of ambition."

A lot of ambition and a market niche that was willing to subscribe.

CARVING OUT THE NICHE

Sometimes the market niche is so small that an inexpensively produced product can capture it without direct mail. Apparently, exploitation film fans are one such market. They will seek out anything on the films they love. Why they love these films is open to question, but they do, and Rick Sullivan's *Gore Gazette*, a four-page monthly newsletter out of Montclair, New Jersey, capitalizes on this gore-loving market niche.

Sullivan is a fast talker. He has an early Beatles-like haircut, which, he insists, is necessary because he's a member of a "sixties mod band" called "The Creeping Pumpkins."

He works full-time for Theatre Management Associates, a film distribution company in Passaic. He landed the job after having been fired from Exxon where he worked as a financial analyst. He had been caught using company envelopes to mail out his *Gore Gazette.* "Monday, they'd call me in and say, 'Let's say the Exxon building gets leveled two years from now. How much would it cost to replace it?'" After graduating from Ramapo State College with a combined major in accounting and cinematography, Sullivan worked for Exxon for nearly five years. Rudy deBlasio, owner of Theatre Management Associates, was a subscriber to the newsletter. He hired Sullivan as his accountant in 1983.

When I walk into Sullivan's office for our meeting he's on the phone talking to a manager of one of the theater's the company distributes to. He's talking about a film called *The Melting Man.* "The one axe murder scene is pretty good," he tells the theater manager. "It has a scene in the shower where he melts on her."

Targeting Fellow Fans

Gore Gazette began in October 1980. The first issues list it as Rick and Rosemary Sullivan's *Gore Gazette,* but Rosemary is dropped from the most recent issues.

"I was always a fan of horror films," Sullivan tells me. "I began to realize how sleazy the horror film industry was. Two years after releasing a film, they'd rerelease the same film with a different title. Some were just very bad movies. In 'Frankenstein's Bloody Terror' there was no Frankenstein, no mention of him, nothing. The movie was about vampires. I'd go to these movies and get beat a lot.

"I wondered if an advisory letter would work. In October 1980, I ran off 200 copies of a free one-page advisory letter and dropped it off at bookstores. I reviewed two films. At the bottom I gave an address where they could send letters. I got 17 letters saying, 'Wow, it's great.' Little by little it grew and grew.

"When I got fired from Exxon, I sat back for about two months. Within that time *Gore Gazette* didn't come out. By this time there were about 300 subscribers. I must have gotten 200 pieces of mail asking what happened. I figured I owed them one last issue, telling them what happened, saying I could only go on doing it if I charged for it. I got $600 before I said 'back in business' to subscribers.

"I got overwhelming support. We now have almost 500 subscribers at $13-a-year for our four-page newsletter, plus a couple thousand more on newsstand sales. I put 4,000 copies out—500 subscribers, 3,500 newsstand. I rarely get more than

1,200 back from Seabreeze Distributors, who distributes for us in New York City and New Jersey."

Sullivan, whose full-time job is still with Theatre Management, grosses around $6,500 a year from newsletter sales. He also sells videocassettes of films to which he either owns the rights or are public domain. From these films, tee-shirts, and poster sales, he grosses another $15,000 a year—without ever spending money on marketing or advertising.

"I have subscribers in 33 states," says Sullivan. "I'm always amazed how they find out about it." Joe Dante, the Hollywood director of "Gremlins" is, according to Sullivan, an avid *Gore Gazette* subscriber, as are other notable film types.

The perserverance of this market niche is emphasized by Sullivan's claim that while he was vacationing in Paris, he stopped in a used bookstore and found they were selling back issues of his publication for $7.50. "Claim" is the operative word here. Sullivan, while he is very willing to share subscriber lists with questioners or to go through back issues, is one of those people who strikes me as never letting a little exaggeration stand in the way of a good story. He's a consummate salesman, an operator. His publication may offend, but his target market keeps renewing and buying all he has to offer.

FOCUSING THE NICHE

There are happy mediums. While the Boston-based Bankers Publishing Company, which has been publishing books for bankers since 1903, has a small potential universe, its books have an average price tag of $35, so it can make a profit off of the market niche.

Bankers serves a very targeted market. "Our market is very well defined in terms of banking professionals," says Karen Kukish Loh, Bankers marketing manager. "The overwhelming majority of them are commercial bankers. In the last year, because of deregulation, we've been more successful in moving books to savings and loans, thrifts, and credit unions, but they still make up less than 10 percent of our market."

Bob Roen, the executive editor of Bankers, adds, "The market is predetermined for us because the company has established itself as the disseminator of printed information for banks and other financial institutions. That's been the direction of the company since its inception in 1903.

The Biggest Buying Niche

"There are approximately 15,000 commercial banks and 4,000 savings and loans, credit unions, and thrifts in the United States. We've found that the biggest buying market in the past, because of the type of product we've been publishing, has been the commercial bank.

"Most commercial banks, 12,000 or so, have $750 million in assets or less. If you say four-fifths of our market falls within that range, then our products have to be geared towards that market."

Recognizing the market niche you're going after is sometimes not enough. Bankers has gone a step further to recognize that there are portions of the market that are not potential book-buyers. "We find that banks under $25 million in assets just don't buy," observes Roen. "So we generally don't advertise to them."

Marketing Messages

Know the specifics of your market niche. The entrepreneur's biggest benefit is knowing who to target, how big the target is, and which segments just don't pay off.

Sell what you have and stand behind it. People who fall into a specific niche can be counted on to be knowledgable, discriminating, and demanding.

Small markets can have big advantages. Specific markets present opportunities such as free membership lists and swaps of mailing lists with others. If the market is pinpointed in detail the creative selling options are often easy to identify.

Don't confuse fleas with mammoths. The specialized niche is small by definition and the entrepreneur's scale must be adjusted to fit.

In the small niche profit on sales rules. Volume is not the bottom line in this market.

Chapter Eleven

Give 'Em What They Want

SOMETHING COOL ABOUT THIS STORE

The Wellmont Theatre, an old elaborately marqueed theater converted to a four-screen first-run movie house on Bloomfield Avenue in Montclair, New Jersey, meshes with an eclectic amalgalm of old New Jersey, new wave/punk, and middle-of-the-road storefronts. Boomerang, a vintage clothing store on this block, leans toward the punk, but it stands out from the punk-type shops here. Keeping the customers satisfied, giving her target market what they want, is what has made Sue Fitzpatrick, who began Boomerang on a $7,000 investment in 1982, successful.

"Our market is college age and teenyboppers," Fitzpatrick explains in the back office of her store. For her 600-square-foot store space, Fitzpatrick pays $600-a-month, plus a utilities bill of around $75-to-$100 a month. She has it leased through 1989. Since the shop was a florist shop originally, there is quite a bit of art deco nature to the area, replete with elaborately tiled floor and stained glass windows.

The store has grown slowly, but sales have increased by 50 percent each year. In 1984, Fitzpatrick estimates sales were around $100,000. Since most of the goods Boomerang sells are consignment items, the cost of stocking an inventory is relatively low. "Take away the consignment, I have about $7,000 in inventory," she says. This inventory includes cards, jewelry, tee-shirts, three-foot Batman cut-outs, stand-up posters of James Dean, rock star Madonna fingerless gloves, and the like. Fitzpatrick is a little surprised at just how quickly the store took off.

"I was a graphic artist," she says as she shuffles papers on her desk, looking for various clips, ads, and stuff to show me. "I thought I'd be back here in the office with a drawing table doing jobs to take up the slack. I remember I needed an average of $75 in sales a day to meet expenses—pay my living expenses, plus increase inventory. It was immediately much higher. Right off we started averaging $700-a-week. Now we sometimes do that on a Saturday.

Staying Hip to Grow

"I never thought I'd appeal to such young kids," Fitzpatrick admits. "I'm trying for a hip, with-it atmosphere. At first, I was afraid to get associated with rock and roll. I wanted to be strictly vintage. I didn't want to be dated. It turned out if I didn't get associated, I wouldn't be able to grow."

Fitzpatrick dresses straight from the racks of her store. Vintage blouse, slacks, shoes that look like they were gleaned from the finest of house sales. Old clothes cool. She's into it. Part of the reason for her success with her market is that this is her lifestyle.

"We were all in the beginning scene of the new wave," she recalls. "In 1977, we were going to the clubs. We're like punks grown up that didn't fit in."

Fitzpatrick can best be described as a punk entrepreneur. Not punk in the sense of a wise guy or a smart aleck, but rather a punk that parallels the "cool," "hip," and, forgive me, "groovy" of another era. She's a businesswoman first; the fun follows. "The drive for me is that this is a personal stake. It's not a candy store. In this type of business you have to convince people there's something cool about this store."

She convinces. The first year she ran an ad video, which ran in Bergen and Essex counties, on MTV, the music video station. "The deal with the 30-second commercial," Fitzpatrick says, "is that it'd be produced for $500, plus I had to buy $1,000 worth of commercials, which turned out to be two months of seven-days-a-week. It turned out to be like $50 a shot. It ran at 11 and 11:30 at night. During the first week, I got a ten-year-old kid running in here with his parents saying, 'There's the place. This is it.'"

She also runs an ad for Boomerang's mail order business in the classified section of *Rolling Stone* magazine, another bastion of coolness.

Creative Window Displays

Boomerang has also exuded "coolness" with its creative window displays, which have included exhibitions by break dancers, and a show put on by models and a grafitti artist. "I took a giant roll-up blind last winter and paid a grafitti artist $10 on a Saturday morning to paint it," she recalls.

"Our windows are known," beams Fitzpatrick. The Montclair Chamber of Commerce bestowed a first place window award on Boomerang for the best window display in its section of Bloomfield Avenue. The display was a vintagely dressed woman mannequin serving a Big Mac to a vintagely dressed man mannequin who was sitting at a table in the window.

Building Status With the Customers

Throughout the week, Boomerang's customers are usually high school kids—12-to-18-years-old. On weekends, they're joined by a college crowd, mostly supplied by the nearby Montclair State.

"I even have mothers coming in shopping for their kids," Fitzpatrick says, smiling. "The majority is local clientele, but they come from Jersey City, Bergen County, Trenton, Morristown, even some people come in from Manhattan." Montclair is about 10 miles outside of New York City.

"I know a lot of these kids by name. I give out free Boomerang buttons. When the kids see each other wear them, it's like status." A lot of the kids also ask her for the labels she uses for bags, so they can stick them on their lockers and bookcovers.

It's about time for Boomerang to open, so Fitzpatrick moves out to the sales area. It's a Friday morning and business won't really start picking up until school's out. Behind the cash register there are some snapshots of some of her customers. On a ledge behind the counter two Boomerang buttons hold a place of honor. "Two of my customers keep their buttons here and put them on when they come in," Fitzpatrick explains. "I keep them here for them." She really likes these kids. And the kids really seem to like the cool Boomerang's offers them.

A mother and small child rap on the door. Fitzpatrick explains that the store won't open for another half-hour. The mother says she'll grab a cup of coffee over at the Montclair Sweet Shop and will be back.

"I get English magazines to make sure I know what's going on," Fitzpatrick says as she relocks the door. She picks up a copy of i-D Magazine, a magazine of British fashion. "Some is so bizarre," she admits, "but it eventually filters down to American fashion. Paisley's big in England now. I have a paisley window now. I want to get rid of the day-glow stuff before I get stuck with it, because by next year it will look so horrible."

Peak Sales

The average sale at Boomerang is between $10 and $15. But at Halloween and Christmas purchase totals jump. "It's jammed in here at Halloween and Christmas. During those two times we do close to 30-to-50 percent of our total business."

While used clothing makes up the major portion of Boomerang's offerings, Fitzpatrick is strictly business when it comes to pricing, and she'll rarely negotiate. "We're low enough as it is. Do you go into Burberry's and try to get something for cheaper?" she asks. Boomerang—the Burberry's of vintage clothing.

Buying Inventory

Fitzpatrick has two regular consignment people who bring her most of the vintage clothes. "They bring in hundreds and hundreds of clothes. They trust me. I usually pay them every week. They're averaging $100-to-$200-a-week.

"I don't go into any thrift shops," Fitzpatrick confides. "I don't want kids to see me and say, 'Oh, what does she do, go to a thrift shop and wash it and put it on the rack?' I like them to think I get the stuff from a secret place."

Boomerang uses the tag "Fashions that keep coming back" in many of its ads. It also has customers who keep coming back. Fitzpatrick has built her business on giving her customers what they want. She keeps up with the funky trends and talks to the kids who patronize her store.

Kids are comfortable coming back to Boomerang. Unlike some other vintage clothing stores, Boomerang is clearly more than a hobby with Fitzpatrick.

Attracting Repeat Business

Giving the market what it wants is important to get it to keep coming back. Rich Melman, whose Lettuce Entertain You Inc., owns Ed Debevic's Short Orders/Deluxe in Chicago, the diner designed to fulfill anyone's dream of diner, says that while Ed's has become the in-vogue place to be for the wealthy and not-so-wealthy alike, once his customers taste the burgers, they'll keep coming back. His assessment appears to be accurate.

Near East Foods, of Leominster, Massachusetts, whose main product is rice pilaf, goes out of its way to make the customer feel comfortable with the product and its other ethnic specialties. Says Walter Moquin, vice president for sales and marketing: "As the brand name becomes comfortable with consumers, they will feel comfortable that, yes, we are an ethnic line, but the product will taste good, too. We try to spend money with the market and the customer in mind. One of our strengths is that people like Procter & Gamble and General Foods develop plans and programs which are usually the same all over. We've really proved our growth in

New England as a working partnership with retailers, food concerns, and the consumer."

Jack Kalajian, president of Near East, adds: "I don't think anything is very ethnic any more. The whole thing changed during the black revolution. The whole American culture did a turnaround at the time. Everyone started feeling good about their ethnic background. I think that our business started to really grow at the time of this ethnic revolution."

ONE STEP AHEAD OF THE CRAZE

Fortunately, Near East was there with products to meet consumer demand when the ethnic revolution hit. In East Grand Forks, Minnesota, Maury Finney, owner of Maury's, an electronics, video, and appliance shop, which did about $1.4 million in gross sales in 1984, is trying to keep up with another consumer revolution—electronics.

"There's no question electronics is going to grow," Finney says. "It seems once something becomes the consumer craze, everybody wants to do it. We have to be one step ahead of the craze."

Maury's started small in 1964. In fact, in the early years, Finney sold color televisions door-to-door. Whenever he'd go in to repair a black and white set, he'd loan a color set. Sales steadily grew.

Confirming the notion that most entrepreneurial spirits are not akin to settling down in one job, Finney also is a crack country and western saxophone player. He won country and western instrumentalist of the year accolades in 1978 from *Record World*, *Cash Box*, and *Billboard* magazines. Finney is 46-years-old, but even with his full head of white hair he looks younger. He's got deep blue eyes and is very businesslike in a grey suit, pink shirt, and striped tie. He loves his business, and giving customers what they want has been the foundation for the growth of Maury's over the last two decades.

Get Into the Market and Be the Best

"When VCRs became the fancy of the consumer," Finney explains, "I decided if we were going to be in the video market, we'd have to be the best. When the CED format from RCA video disk started around three years ago, we immediately went into purchasing and selling videodisk players and movies. We carried every title and continue to carry every title. We put a rental package together at the time. No one in the area was doing it, so we just had to factor out the cost. You know, sell the shaver cheap and rent the blades. We were renting disks out as far as Montana."

When RCA decided to discontinue making the disk player, rather than panic, which Finney must have done to some degree, he bought up as many players as he could for the rental operation. He thought he had a corner on the market. But he also realized he had to move his customers into the videocassette recorder (VCR) market as well.

"The VCR market has stabilized little by little," observes Finney. "We've got about 350 titles we're renting out now and are increasing all the time. We're also continuing to buy the disks as long as they make them."

Unique Market Demands

The Midwest market has also created a demand unique to the area. Because there are many open areas, television reception is not too keen everywhere. In 1982, Finney decided to branch out into the satellite dish market, which he seems to have a corner on in the area. To date, the market is still small, but Finney boasts about $150,000 in sales of satellite dishes alone each year since he started his company.

"We handle one line from Kansas called the 'Birdview' line. In the last year, prices have dropped 30 percent. A complete satellite dish system installed now costs around $3,300 for a top-of-the-line system. Other systems go for less than a thousand, but they only pick up some transmissions."

Again, Finney hopes he's one step ahead of the satellite dish craze. His track record at guessing right is good. From 1971 to 1976, Maury's was instrumental in strongly promoting the microwave oven to its market. "For a while we were doing 60 percent of the market," Finney says. "The microwave oven was a godsend. What gave us the volume was that my wife has given free microwave oven classes every month to customers. In fact she just gave one last night. She's in her eleventh year of microwave classes."

The satellite dish market is rural. To introduce the market to the product, Finney had a four-color brochure with a letter inserted into a newspaper that hit the market.

"The letter explained our position—that we had been in the service business for years. We told them we had examined and critiqued the satellite business, and we invited them to the store to see it. It was a good kickoff, a beautiful brochure. For several weeks, potential buyers would come in with the brochure."

Fighting the Chains by Offering Service

Maury's has grown because it has satisfied customer desires and then some. The company faces constant competition from the large discount houses which can undersell Finney because of large volume capacity. Maury's only has 4,800 square feet of front sales area, a service area of 4,000 square feet, and a warehouse next door of 2,400 square feet. A year-and-a-half ago Maury's joined a Minnesota buying group so it could, says Finney, "buy products cheaper and handle the chains." But the service Maury's can give undercuts anything the large chains can offer.

"The chains are more irksome than anything elese," he says. "Sometimes they will dump something on the market that we are in the process of merchandising. Sometimes people don't consider the services we offer and that does hurt us. But it's not as tough as those wholesale catalogs with WATS lines that people bring in to show us. Most times we can turn it into a retail sale if we sit them down and tell them about our service. The warranty's only as good as the service that backs it."

On a cool night in East Grand Forks, Minnesota, Maury Finney can rest in his easy chair, and sometimes, if the wind is blowing just right, he can pick up a Nashville radio station playing his 1976 recording of "Maiden's Prayer," with the Lea Jane Singers singing the chorus, and Finney mellowly blowing out the tune that hit the country and western number one spot on the charts. He gave them what they wanted and his tunes hit number one. Over the last couple of decades, Maury's has taken the same tack, with, Finney hopes, similar results.

Consistency

Small businesspeople, entrepreneurs like Maury Finney, who are running businesses successfully know that to continue succeeding the market must be given what it wants with some level of consistency. Not garbage one week and gladiolas the next, but desired products or services throughout.

Stephen Garber, owner of the London Wine Company, in Brookline, Massachusetts, knows this as well as anyone. Through his use of direct mail software called The Correspondent (produced by the Selkirk Associates), he can track his customers' likes and dislikes. "We try to provide a unique service by offering wines to suit individual tastes," says Garber. "Unlike the trial and error method of sales.

Bill's Florist in the Del's Village shopping center in Boonton, New Jersey, also understands the importance of giving the market what it wants. "Every flower shop in every town is differnt," Dennis Goldenberg, who owns Bill's with his father, Herb, tells me in his basement office. "People go to a particular flower shop because they like what they do."

Since buying the shop in 1973, Bill's Florist's gross sales have multiplied more than tenfold. "In 1973 and 1974, sales were $45,000. In December of 1984 alone, we did $70,000," Dennis says.

"We cater to a different clientele than our Boonton competition," he insists. "The people we cater to are Boonton Township, Mountain Lakes people, a more affluent market. Our selection is more diverse. It's more like a New York shop. Most of our customers are business executives who commute to New York." Boonton is a 45-minute drive from Manhattan.

"We have the European market—fewer flowers, more stylish, more in line with the trend style. We like to think we've Americanized the European, taking styles we like and incorporating them into what we offer."

FRAMING THE MARKET

Bill's Florist is growing at the rate of 20-to-25 percent a year in gross sales, by offering more than just voluminous bunches of mums or carnations. Dennis and Herb Goldenberg like to think they're selling an attitude which exudes style, current trends, and market desires.

It's tough to be unique and still meet the demands of the market. Outline Inc., a Walpole, Massachusetts-based manufacturer of lightweight trade show exhibit systems, has managed to grow to a $9 million-plus business in five short years by giving the market what it wants, but didn't know it needed.

"We're in a very traditional marketplace," says David Gilvar, Outline's president, referring to the tradeshow display industry. "But we approach the market in a unique way."

The unique way Outline approaches the market is that, unlike its competitors, it doesn't try to sell the system hardware as much as it tries to sell the message that the system hardware can convey. As a result, Outline not only manufactures the aluminum hardware, but also the graphics that the buyers will use to display their messages. Gilvar says that about 60 percent of sales are graphics plus hardware, while 40 percent are just hardware alone. "We don't sell the frames," says Gilvar. "The frames come along with the message."

Outline now has showrooms in seven markets, including Waltham, Massachusetts, Chicago, New York, Dallas, Los Angeles, Ft. Lauderdale, and Philadelphia. "Our long-range marketing plan is that the regional offices will open satellite showrooms," says Gilvar.

The client list for Outline is impressive, made up of companies like Estee Lauder, Montgomery Ward, American Airlines, Mazda, and AT&T. The Outline-supplied frames and graphics are not only being used for tradeshows, but also as free-standing in-store displays and window displays. Sears Financial Network bought several Outline systems to use as window displays to introduce the financial network during its expansion. American Express used several systems with graphics of the Statue of Liberty for a traveling exhibit to gain public support for the Statue's reconditioning over the next year-and-a-half.

Mazda is using three of the systems as earnings boards and scoreboards for the Ladies Professional Golf Association tour they're sponsoring. "They're [the Outline display systems] going to be used outdoors, which is something new for us," Gilvar says. Mazda is "so happy . . . they're talking about using [our system] in all their showrooms."

According to Gilvar, Estee Lauder's "Clinique" sales in Pittsburgh "went up 100 percent using our displays." Prompting Estee Lauder, of course, to come back and place "a really big order."

Selling Solutions to Problems

The customer list grows and grows, and keeps coming back for more display systems because Outline is able to give its customers solutions to problems, both in display and design. Tell them what they want and then sell it to them in carloads has been Outline's approach.

The hardware of Outline's system sells from around $1,000 and up, depending on what features (e.g., tables, lamps, computerized message boards) the buyer chooses. The graphics range widely in price, depending upon complexity.

As Outline gains a stronger foothold into the in-store market, a market which is virtually untapped by anybody in the industry according to Gilvar, potential for growth is astronomical. While some of the bigger chain stores may only order a few systems for each of their outlets, the fact that chains such as Montgomery Ward and Sears have hundreds of stores spells multiple purchases. And not just one time purchases, either. While the hardware can be used over and over again, new graphics panels can be designed and purchased from Outline each season to reflect new fashions or products. An ideal situation for Outline to be able to continue giving the market more of what it wants, over and over again, with gusto.

Marketing Messages

Focus on the market and give it what it wants. This is the key to entrepreneurial success. When the market knows where to go to get what it wants—and needs—it keeps coming back for more.

Consistency, consistency, consistency: The Three Cs of holding on to your market. You can't have gladiolas one week and garbage the next. The Three Cs are a magnet to future sales.

Offer the best. Tell customers why you're special, different from the competition. Give the market solutions to its problems.

Chapter Twelve

Dissecting the Segment

"It's fun in here. You can see everybody walking by," Bob Daniels tells me in the conference room of Project Software Development Inc.'s (PSDI) posh new Charles Square offices, in Cambridge, Massachusetts. This is a far cry from the $125-a-month basement office Daniels occupied by himself a few blocks away when he founded the company in 1968.

"I was a research engineer at MIT in the civil engineering department," recalls Daniels. "I became interested in computerized project management techniques at MIT." When he graduated, Daniels' work became public domain, and it became the basis for PSDI's first software product, a high-priced project management system. "The stuff from MIT was more-or-less useless, but it was a starting point."

PROJECT/2 is the name of the software. It is a project management system which is tailored to a customer's needs and sells for between $250,000 and $750,000. In its fiscal year, 1984, gross sales for PSDI, which now employs 250 people, were around $20 million.

Marketing to Middle Management

PSDI targeted a market successfully, a top-dollar paying market at that. But Daniels wasn't satisfied. "In late 1983, we tried to decide what to do in terms of future products," he says. "It finally dawned on us that the IBM-PC was the target for a new product. We decided that the only way to handle these other companies getting at our throats was to transport our expertise to the level of the average manager. We decided to go after this market."

Not a new market, really, but a different portion of the same market PSDI had been hitting all along. This time instead of high-price tailored software to top management, the market was middle-management and the software was an IBM-PC compatible package called QWIKNET, retailing for $895. "It's called downward marketing," to coin a phrase and kill the language.

"We expect some of our big customers to buy hundreds of copies of QWIKNET at $895," says Daniels. "We're specialists. We don't try to do anything more than what we're good at—project management and tools for project management."

QWIKNET, which started being shipped on January 1, 1985, has sold a couple of thousand copies. Daniels estimates that currently PSDI is taking in around $160,000-a-month selling the product. "We're now building our sales and distribution channels," he says.

To take care of customers that already leased PROJECT/2 and have now purchased copies of QWIKNET, PSDI is about to introduce a link between the two which will allow information to be uploaded from QWIKNET to PROJECT/2. "Our new ad campaign will emphasize the two working together. QWIKNET and PROJECT/2 are a hell of a team," Daniels says.

No Fear of the Competition

"When we made the decision in August of 1983 to put together a team to develop QWIKNET, it was done as well as we've done anything. By five months out, we were well-engaged into systems programming. Within nine months, we had the prototype.

Within a year, we released the preliminary software. After 16 months, we went commercial with version 2."

Daniels estimates there are 40 or 50 microcomputer competitors that offer project management software competitive with QWIKNET. It doesn't phase him. "Our product is so good that regardless of competitors entering the market, and in spite of the fact that at $895 we're more expensive that seven-eighths of our competitors, we'll be successful."

The introduction of the QWIKNET software, which comes bundled with a "mouse," has not been flawless, however. The preliminary release of version 1 was, in Daniels opinion, a mistake. "It was reviewed by someone who did not shed enough favorable light on the product. When we delivered version 2 in January 1985, however, it had outstanding reviews."

The central ordering division for the retail computer chain, Computerland, refuses to carry QWIKNET because of the price. "They strongly suggested we sell to individual Computerland stores, which we do."

Overall, Daniels believes the "micro thing" is going well.

Full-Fledged Ad Campaign

To launch QWIKNET, the company spent $500,000 in advertising from November 1984 to March 1985. Two full-page ads in *The Wall Street Journal* run on election day and the day after alone cost PSDI more than $100,000. Daniels is quick to point out that "We got 600, maybe 700 inquiries from those two ads."

From the leads generated by the ads, PSDI is starting to do some direct mail for QWIKNET. "We have a data base of around 10,000 names from the ads that hasn't really been worked," says Daniels. "We're starting to work it now."

QWIKNET also has two full-time telemarketing people, a supervisor, and five customer support people. "We make enough money on a copy to provide some support to the customer. We get 15-to-20 calls daily for assistance from customers, which is good. We can handle that with no problem."

Grooming Customers Upward

The dissection of the target is not limited to QWIKNET. The company is now working on an advanced version of QWIKNET, which will cost between $2,000 and $3,000. The hope is that customers will be groomed upward to the more expensive PROJECT/2 software.

PSDI is also working on a new software product designed for plant management. It will help keep track of maintenance and equipment in industrial facilities. It'll be released for $18,000, the hefty price tag resulting from Daniels perception that there's no competition and it's a major vertical niche. "It's a major commitment for us. We presented it at the National Plant Maintenance Show in Chicago in March 1985. A number of people were interested in it." The plant management software will be called MAXIMO.

Broader Market Potential

The interesting result of PSDI's dissection of its own market niche is that it doesn't always result in smaller parts. QWIKNET, for example, because of its price and its simpler applications, will have a much broader market potential than PROJECT/2 or any of the higher ticket software products PSDI is marketing. It's also impressive that Daniels and his crew are able to make everything seem to work together so well.

Daniels introduces his assistant, Amy Kipp, a tall, slender, red-haired woman with freckles. Kipp is an indication of why things seem to mesh so well at PSDI. On several occassions prior to this meeting with Daniels, Kipp has been able to get me information, answers, suggestions, and most everything I needed to prepare for my discussion. From talking with dozens of business people around the country, I find that the Kipps are few.

Daniels reminds me, "We're technically terrific. I believe businesses should complement each other. One thing powers the other and vice-versa. And you get this momentum. It's very important that everything fit together. The trick is to make one thing improve the other's position in the market to the point of actual impact."

Judging from the introduction of QWIKNET, which Daniels believes will easily add $2 million in sales to PSDI in 1985, and $5 million the following year, the trick is working.

Marketing Messages

Do what you do best and stick with it. When you're dissecting a market with a new product make sure that product complements your exisitng business.

If it fits, it works. Everything should mesh together, ideas powering ideas, products powering new products. The result is momentum and a bigger market.

Major markets are made up of many smaller ones. Focus, dig deep into your market base. The perceptive entrepreneur can mine new gold that leads to further growth.

Maxim Four

The Presentation Principle

Capture the Market With Captivating Concepts. Use the *Right* Method for Your Message.

How's the marketplace to know about a product or service without a presentation? Word-of-mouth is often a crucial marketing tool, but even then it's important that the word-of-mouth presents a product or service in a favorable light. For many of the businesses profiled in the following chapters, presenting their product gives them one of their most interesting marketing challenges. After all, if the presentation doesn't cause the potential market to see the product in a favorable light, why would anybody want to buy what these businesses have to offer?

There are many ingredients that go into successful product presentation. Often it's something as simple as a corporate identity or logo. If you sell a product that promises to make other businesses look good, that promise, to succeed, had better be packaged in a good-looking brochure with an equally good-looking logo on it. Corporate identity that is carried over into all of a company's sales materials is as important as anything else that goes into product presentation.

Advertising—whether it be through newspapers, television, or direct mail—is also critical to a successful product presentation. Getting just the right message across in a campaign, one with which the marketplace can identify, can be the key ingredient in business taking off. Consider, for example, the "Mary Campaign" (Chapter 14) that Victory Shirts launched quite successfully, giving its market of upscale shirt buyers a clear idea that when they bought a shirt from Victory, they weren't only buying the shirt; they were buying the commitment of the company's president. Or look at how a jewelry store in Madison, Wisconsin, by working closely with its advertising agency to create an innovative television advertising campaign, has been able to distinguish itself as different from the jewelry stores and department stores which crowd its market.

Businesses are able to create some word-of-mouth marketing by offering seminars as educational forums to a marketplace that potentially would be interested in purchasing what they have to offer. Add some solid public relations effort to that, and the word spreads quite quickly about who the movers and shakers in the marketplace are.

Staging special events has also helped many of the businesses present a product. Special events not only give the perception that a business might be doing a public service by offering expositions, it also draws people back for more information or products. Special events have the added attraction of stimulating sales. During a business' off-peak season this can be an incredibly attractive marketing tool.

Everybody has heard the cliche that you can't judge a book by its cover. But it's often forgotten that an attractive cover can make you *want* to read. In the following pages you'll learn how entrepreneurs use an appealing cover to attract a market—and keep it.

Chapter Thirteen

Corporate Identity: Painting a Clearer Picture

It was an ironic paradox. David Gilvar and David Burr had built a hugely successful business helping other companies to project the right image. But now the growth of their own company was threatened by the image it projected.

Their product, a lightweight, versatile trade show exhibit system called "Outline," had done well, with sales climbing from $260,000 in 1980 to $2.5 million in 1982. One of the keys to that success was the decision in early 1982 to shift from offering the hardware alone to offering finished exhibits, with client-designed panels installed in the folding framework.

That meant trying to reach the design "specifiers" at ad agencies or corporate marketing departments who would incorporate the Outline system into the exhibit designs they prepared. But in going after that market, Outline's sales staff actually had to battle against the image that company put forth in its sales literature.

Outline Inc., then called Extraversion, Inc., wanted to present itself as a graphically sophisticated company and attract a design-conscious buyer. But the image the company projected, from its logo through all of its promotional material, was still that of a hardware manufacturer relatively unconcerned about graphic presentation.

"Our brochures and literature were the type of thing that any design-oriented person would probably throw in the wastepaper basket," recalls Gilvar, chairman of the Waltham, Massachusetts-based Outline. "[The salespeople] would make a demonstration and the customer would say that's the greatest thing he's ever seen. But our salesmen would leave behind this terrible brochure that was, if anything, detrimental to marketing. Or they'd call up a vice president of marketing, who'd say 'Send me a brochure. If I like what I see, I'll make an appointment.' Then they'd send this terrible brochure and they'd never get in the door."

Deciding on a Complete Graphic Redesign

In late 1982, Gilvar and Burr, Outline's president, decided that what the company needed was not just a new brochure, but a complete graphic redesign that would put the company's image in tune with its market. The makeover took more than a year to complete, but it has given Outline's marketing a powerful boost. "We are now getting to people who I'm sure were not in our corner at all with the older version of our marketing pieces," says one Outline executive. Revenues in 1984 hit $9 million.

"We knew that if we could ever communicate to people that our product was that good and that we had something that would really make people's lives much easier and they could really use it ... if we came up with a promotional piece that could do that, we'd be off and running," Gilvar says as we walk through the production area of Outline's Walpole, Massachusetts, plant. "We didn't have anything that did that, but we knew we had a product that was unique and could be sold throughout the United States—not a $9 million company, but a $100 million company."

Finding the Right Design Firm

So, in December 1982, Outline began a search for a design firm. The task was beyond the reach of its in-house graphics staff. "Within our framework, there's no one on staff that's involved in a day-to-day corporate identity program," says David Peck, manager of Outline's visual services.

It wasn't easy to find the right firm. Ouline began by checking out some of the bigger design houses in New York. "We knew, however, that when push came to shove, we'd be 53rd on the totem pole in terms of priority," says Burr.

"These big firms were trying to sell us on a new look and a new fancy brochure, a fancy mailing piece, a fancy logo. But they never identified with us and our marketing problems and goals," says Gilvar. "They didn't make us feel like we would be part of the creative process and that our ideas would be valued."

Finally, they discovered a communications design firm that seemed to suit their needs: Lapham/Miller Associates of Andover, Massachusetts. "They said to us, 'Now, we'll have to sit down and learn about your company, your customers, and your competition so that we can solve that communications problem,'" says Gilvar. "We said, 'Okay, let's talk about it.'"

During that initial meeting in February 1983, "We spent about 85 percent of the time talking about their product," recalls Ken Miller, president of Lapham/Miller, whose offices in Andover are located in the restored Chickering House, now a registered National Historical Landmark. "Their enthusiasm was infectious. We became equally excited about what we could do for them."

There were three more preliminary meetings in which Miller and Ralph Lapham, vice president of the design firm, probed further into Outline's market, goals, and problems. "They got into our heads and found out exactly what our problems were, what we wanted to accomplish," says Gilvar.

A Complete Graphic Makeover

Lapham/Miller proposed a thorough graphic makeover, including a new logo, a new brochure and a mailer—the first in the company's history. Gilvar and Burr gave the okay, launching a series of intensive meetings with the designers.

Through those meetings, Gilvar and Burr hammered out with Lapham/Miller a whole new identity for Outline—a more consistent, sophisticated look with an entirely new approach to presenting the product. "Traditionally, people in our industry show what they produced for other people," explains Gilvar. "The idea of being able to sell our message without peddling the greatest exhibit we just did for Sears or American Express was the direction we decided to go."

Miller explains that his company had to present Outline's exhibit system as a tasteful complement to an end user or design specifier and stimulate interest in the various configurations. "We wanted the end user to dream along with its possibilities. There's very little of 'Put tab A into slot B,' which to all of us distinguished Outline's product from the competition," he says.

As the generic graphic display on the exhibit system, it was decided to use the image of a lemon as Outline's initial theme. "We tried to show that if we could sell something as generic as a lemon and make it attractive, prospective customers could make their own judgment about carrying the system," Miller recalls.

"We were in and out of 10-to-15 meetings with them, doing sketches, then coming back and forth with new ideas," says Lapham. "We must have tried at least 100 different approaches, all of them with the idea that it would be clean, with a kind of Germanic-European look, primarily playing with the most important part of the exhibit, the unfolding part of it."

Lapham took those ideas and translated them into a logo and a capabilities brochure using the lemon premise. The final product went to the printer in March 1984. Other than the colors of the lemons, the brochure's chief colors are mauve and gray, "very contemporary colors in the design and architecture world," according to Lapham. The direct mail piece has the same look as the brochure, carrying out the theme of making a lemon look good. Even Outline's sales offices were painted the same mauve and gray to reflect the new identity.

Overhaul Success

Outline's direct mail piece is intended to generate leads for the sales staff. The first mailing was dropped in June 1984, and the company plans to mail to a different segment of the market each month. Says David Peck: "One week after it had been dropped, out of the 25 responses we've received a day, four or five would have something extraneous written on the bottom of the card, like 'Keep up this great image.'"

Costs

The overhaul didn't come cheap. After a year-and-a-half, Outline ran up a tab of nearly $150,000 with Lapham/Miller, including production and printing costs. But companies interested in a new graphic image needn't shell out that kind of cash.

"Outline made a major commitment on a national budget," says Miller. "We've got loads of clients with smaller budgets." To initiate and complete overhaul, Miller believes a minimum financial commitment should be in the $25,000 range. Lapham/ Miller has, however, dealt with companies where the commitment has only been in the $10,000 range.

New Identity to Attract New Markets

Some companies do not require a complete overhaul. Robert Cox, vice president of Walsh Brothers, a contracting firm in Cambridge, Massachusetts, wanted Lapham/Miller to design a brochure that would "present an image of Walsh Brothers that would be more acceptable to the private industry."

For 80 years, Walsh Brothers had been doing business basically by word-of-mouth. Much of its business has been in the educational and institutional market, but the firm wanted to attract private industry as well. After going through a familiarization process with Lapham/Miller, a brochure was designed incorporating dramatic photography that displays Walsh Brothers' credentials.

The response to the brochure was phenomenal. According to Miller, "They got so much business from it they boxed the brochures and put them away."

"We still use the brochure when we have to, but we're not out scouring the market for work," says Cox. "As a matter of fact, we pulled back. We've had too much work. We had hoped the brochure would be a catalyst for the private industry to call back and say, 'We'd like to talk to you.' It worked."

Going for that "Pro Look"

Brent Marmo, president of The Brownstone Group, a design studio in Brookline, Massachusetts, that specializes in corporate identity programs, is completing work with Colortek, a professional color lab in Boston that reports about $1 million-a-year in sales of everything from color murals to color prints. Colortek wanted a more professional look to capture the corporate market. Marmo's work resulted in a new logo, letterhead, business cards, and a new marketing piece.

The Design Process

Like Lapham/Miller, Marmo likes to take his clients through a "design process." The first step is the initial research and design which typically takes two-to-three weeks. This involves gathering relevant information, generating options, and selecting a general approach for the logo.

At the end of the three weeks, the presentation of the basic format of the piece(s) is made, including a color palate and typography. The final mock-up of the graphics piece comes two weeks later. Add one-to-three weeks, depending on the complexity, after the mock-up for production work to be completed. Finally, if the client is satisfied, the mechanical is sent to the printer.

Colortek expects to pay The Brownstone Group just under $10,000 for design, production, and printing of the direct mail piece, letterhead, business cards, envelopes, and a few other pieces. Just over $3,000 of this is for Brownstone's design and production services; the remainder is for printing.

Although the final cost is less than a tenth of what Outline spent, for Colortek it represents a major commitment. Says Mimi Rancatore, general manager of Colortek: "We decided this was the time to invest. If we really wanted to expand our business and get more corporate accounts, this was the way we had to approach it."

Investing in a "Look"

Marmo points out that a client can spend less money and get a beautiful—or at least an adequate—image from a free-lancer. "But I think the people who realize they need a look for their company are also businesspeople. They realize it's an investment and they need it."

Working with a design/communications firm like Lapham/Miller or Brownstone is a handsome alternative to an expensive advertising firm for the smaller, entrepreneurial business which might not be ready to foot a hefty advertising bill. The identity and collateral material that design firms can offer are often more crucial for a new or growing business' successful entry into new markets.

Colortek will incur a lower cost than Outline because of its limited needs and the size of the print runs. The quality of the work and its effectiveness in positioning Colortek to meet its goal of going after a corporate market are on par with Outline's efforts. "This is a nice, handsome piece," says Rancatore. "You get a lot of garbage in the mail. This brochure is something that I would find hard to throw away. It also houses original film and prints—something I've never seen. It shows what we can produce."

Gilvar is also enthusiastic about the results of Outline's graphic overhaul. "It's been tremendously successful," he says. "But it's the quality of the response we're getting that's most important. The brochures have given us tremendous credibility. None of our stuff gets thrown in the wastebasket.

"Now, when we leave a piece behind at an advertising agency, it is well received. We're working on a big order for Estee Lauder in their Clinique area. Now a graphic designer working for a cosmetic company thinks if we're chic, we can make them look chic."

MARKETING MESSAGES

Corporate image mirrors your product. The way you look solves a lot of communications problems. It tells the market what it can expect from your company.

When it comes to image-making, be part of the process. Look for a design company that makes you a part of the creative process. Work with it to examine the market, your needs, and any problems with current corporate identity.

Why the new look? Determine the underlying goal of the identity you're seeking. New images need motives if they are to work for you.

Chapter Fourteen

Using Newspaper Advertising: The Mary Campaign

"Tie one on free at Victory," reads the ad on the bottom of page two of Monday's *New York Times.* Advertising a free silk tie with every three cotton men's or women's shirts purchased is a far cry from pouring through a shirt inventory of purples, stripes, and assorted "fancies" down on Orchard Street, just off Delancey, in the garment district of Manhattan.

Mary Sprague, who took over Victory Shirt Company in November 1984, now likes to think that the quality of her goods goes head-to-head with Brooks Brothers and the finest shirt stores in town. With three stores in New York City, and two in suburban Washington, D.C. (Fairfax, Virginia and north Bethesda, Maryland), Sprague has successfully grown a fledging shirt company into well over a $1 million-a-year operation, which employs more than 30 people. Just how much over a million is difficult to assess. When you ask Sprague, she'll take out another cigarette, light it, and say, "Let's see, now where were we?"

She had no retail experience when she purchased Victory. At the time her interest was piqued, she was doing graduate work in literature at Sarah Lawrence. When she found Victory was for sale, she thought she could make a go of it. Over the decade or so that has passed since she took over Victory Shirts, she has used her marketing savvy to transform Victory into a very successful business.

The effective use of print advertising has certainly set her apart from the crowd. So has her commitment to offering quality shirts that are made better and sell for less than the competition.

The history of Victory's print advertising has been one that couples naivete with an implicit sense of marketing know-how. Sprague is an entrepreneur who is willing to take risks, and her judgment calls usually prove correct. Like all business people who have successfully grown small operations into large, successful ones, Sprague realizes there are trade-offs and rocky times are expected. "Corporately we're profitable," she says. "But had I chosen to stay small we would have been much more profitable."

Victory's midtown store is at the corner of 44th and Madison, nestled between the Elite Deli Pizza Restaurant and a Camera Barn. Just across the street is the behemoth Brooks Brothers New York store. Sprague's office is located on a second floor loft area overlooking the inventory and sales area. I'm a little early for our morning meeting, so I sit in a chair facing her ornate desk and breathe in the steam from the coffee one of the Victory people gave me. Awake by inhalation. On the bookcase behind Sprague's desk there's a collection of books ranging from Betty Friedan's *Second Stage* to Robert Ludlum's *Parsifal Mosaic* to *Executive Compensation Alert.* Eclectic tastes to fit the entrepreneur.

Mary Sprague is a slender woman who speaks very clearly and evenly. She is clearly driven by her business, but the pictures hanging on the wall behind her desk clearly indicate the importance her family plays in her life. I remember Hal Gershman, who owns Happy Harry's Bottle Shop in Grand Forks, North Dakota, telling me: "If you have to build an empire at the expense of your family, I don't think you're building much." Many of the people I've spoken with about marketing and their businesses share his sentiment, and Mary Sprague is one of them.

Deciding a Market Direction

Some businesses can rely on consumers to take it upon themselves to look for ads when they're in the market to buy a particular product. Not so in the shirt industry. And when Mary Sprague took over Victory shirts, she certainly had her work cut out for her.

"The business was very old line and had been let go," Sprague recalls. "The previous owner never kept any kind of records and was looking to get out. He had a dated inventory, with shirts cut for a short, heavy man. Men are trimmer now."

When Sprague bought Victory shirts, she was buying the name and the inventory. "There was no basic inventory. All fancies. No whites and blues. The first thing I had to do was to fix that inventory. In order to do that I had to have a market direction," she says. "The original store was on Orchard Street, where the consumer is upscale, value-conscious. The store wasn't hitting that crowd, so I hired a manufacturer to redesign the body pattern."

Sprague took on the store in November 1974 and wanted to be ready for the Christmas season. No easy task. She found needlework people in Pennsylvania and raised the prices of the shirts Victory offered. As a result, Victory did lose some of its older customers, but it was beginning to aim at a new upscale market. To try to keep as much of the older market as possible, Sprague hired an old Jewish man who spoke Yiddish to help her convince the vintage customers to stick with her.

"We worked side-by-side in the first years," Sprague recalls. "I did all the purchasing. He helped with selling. That first Christmas I ran a 'buy one, get one free' sale to get rid of [the previous owner's] inventory. I was able to offer the value-conscious consumer a deal.

"I can remember having an $800 Sunday around that Christmas and thinking it was astronomical. I couldn't turn on the lights at Madison Avenue for that."

Using Ads to Move Inventory

Victory made it through that first Christmas with shirts supplied by the needlework people in Pennsylvania. But by July of 1975, Sprague faced a new crisis. "I got a big shipment in in July of 1975. I was concerned because the plant had 10-day terms for labor. I wanted to move the shirts quickly enough to pay the plant." Cash flow in July in retail in New York City is tough; many of Sprague's competitors thought her hopelessly optimistic to think she could move a big shipment at the slowest time of year. "I didn't want to promote the merchandise and give it away and lose my margin," she remembers.

The solution opened the book on Victory's long relationship with successful print advertising. "I designed an ad and put it in *New York* magazine," says Sprague. "That was my first advertising. I did it as a mail order, with a coupon. We offered a very basic cotton men's shirt in four colors. No credit cards. You had to send a check. The typeface was totally wrong and you couldn't tell from the art what the shirt looked like. I carried the mechanical personally to *New York* magazine's office and placed the ad."

In spite of its shortcomings, the ad offering the $13 shirts pulled well. In the first couple of days, Victory got a couple of hundred orders. "I didn't even have enough shipping cartons," smiles Sprague. "I didn't expect that kind of return."

Because she had plenty of stock on hand, she shipped right away and was able to pay off the manufacturer.

The "Bounceback Concept"

As a result of this first *New York* experience, Sprague also discovered another marketing avenue.

"I had shipped to an attorney in California who wrote back asking us what kind of operation we were that didn't enclose additional literature with the packaged shirt. Thus, the 'bounceback concept' was born. Now we had two ways to market."

When customers asked how to get on Victory's mail order list, Sprague figured she should start some sort of mail order operation so she'd have a list to add names to. "I saw a printer and put together a black-and-white mailer. On every mailer piece, I stapled a swatch of cotton cloth. My children and I sat at our dining room table stapling the swatches that would give the feel of the cotton. I sent it out to my retail and mail order names."

Sprague placed a clipboard at the Orchard Street store for retail customers to write down their names and addresses. At the same time, she put another ad in *New York* with better photography and appropriate typeface.

Ads Increase Retail Volume

"It was early 1976, and at this point I was taking credit card orders," Sprague recalls. "Everything I did up to this point I thought was wonderful." She ran an ad in *The Wall Street Journal* around this time. People came into the store holding the mail order piece they received, having checked off the swatch they wanted. There was retail response, too. "I could see the retail volume shoot up after the mail order."

She says the ads in *The Wall Street Journal* paid for themselves. "We weren't in there as frequently as the consumers thought we were. The repetition every 10 days was having an impact."

The "Panic Factor"

When the new entrepreneur finds that marketing through logical means is successful, there sometimes comes a point when an inner voice whispers: "It can't be this easy. The consumer's going to catch on that I'm doing this through seat-of-the-pants marketing logic." Panic sets in. In 1977, Sprague faced it.

"I got frightened," she recalls. "I felt the mail order had tremendous potential. I thought I needed professional help. It was going to get big and I was going to make mistakes. I went to a top-flight mail order house in New York in early 1977. We did a four-color catalog, played up the fiftieth anniversary of the business."

Everything promised success. For the first time, Sprague put the controls in the hands of "experts." The result: "It was an unmitigated disaster. The catalog was hard to read and follow. To read the order form you would have needed an engineering degree. The photography was boring. The color was not true, and the layout was garbled. It was an unwieldy size." Sprague puts out her cigarette, places both hands on her desk, and sits back. "I lost a lot on that catalog."

Fortunately, at the time, she was just about to open her Madison Avenue outlet, so she wasn't stuck with the inventory that had been built up for the expected smash mail order results. It was the first time she experienced a loss on something used to promote the business. "It made me mail order shy."

Confidence in Instincts

Like most business owners, Sprague knows that success comes by learning from mistakes. She is no longer in awe of experts. She knows her business and what it takes to make it grow. If an "expert" vendor can't give her what she wants, she now knows there are plenty more to choose from.

From 1974 to 1977, Victory experienced better than 40 percent growth in sales a year. When the Madison Avenue store opened, overhead shot way up, but so did sales. Victory also did very well during the recession of the early 1980s by attracting the fallout from the department stores. "They'd come to Orchard Street and save six bucks without sacrificing any quality."

By 1978, Sprague felt she needed a presence in the financial district. She opened in March 1978 on 10 Maiden Lane. This proved to be another marketing challenge for which she turned to print advertising.

"This is a highly promotional, competitive industry," she explains. "There was a Syms [off-price clothes store] there. It was an area where the customer was tied far more to a telephone. They were time-conscious and needed instant care. We were located on a side street so we had to figure out a way to get them in our door."

Special Ad Sales Capture the Market

The answer was a special series of ads in *The New York Times* honoring specials at all three stores but aimed mostly at the market in the financial district. Victory ran a "Stockbrokers Week" offering 20 percent off if the stockbroker customer gave Sprague a business card. There were other "weeks"—"Woman Executives Week," "Bankers Week." It hurt the profit margin a bit, but the "weeks" helped Victory capture the market—and the names of customers for future mailings.

In late 1978, Sprague searched for a new ad agency, a search which ultimately led into a newspaper advertising campaign more successful than she ever could have imagined.

"We felt our ad agency at the time was not doing a very good job," says Sprague. "Our ads were not distinctive. We were spending money but not getting great recognition for our three stores in New York City. We began the search for an agency. I decided whoever got the account would get it on creativity."

A New Look—"The Mary Campaign"

The winning agency was Cappiello and Chabrawe, a Manhattan agency. Tony Cappiello handled the creative end. Terry Chabrawe wrote copy. Tony and Terry decided that for Victory to separate itself beyond value and price, it needed a new look. "They decided *I* was the look," says Sprague. And the "Mary Campaign" was born.

"The first ad was very gutsy," recalls Sprague, who still insists she wasn't too keen on the idea of appearing in her store's ads. "It read: 'Mary's reputation is at stake.' That ad said, 'Here's somebody who's out there knocking the socks off the big guys.' It was written in the first person." The ad shows Mary, arms folded, wearing a Victory shirt, staring straight-on into the camera. The tag line: "My goal is simple. I want to give you the best possible shirt at the lowest possible price."

At the same time, Cappiello and Chabrawe worked the Mary Campaign into Victory's mail order catalog. Catalog requests jumped. Sales, after the campaign was introduced, jumped 20 percent.

The Mary Campaign went out full force with lots of plays on the first ad: "I'd love a chance to dress you." "Why 33,332 men depend on Mary." "Mary put the shirt on my back." "Mary will have you in (the finest) stitches."

"I got lots of interesting mail," says Sprague, "particularly when we ran the one saying 'I'd like to dress you.' More propositions than proposals, really."

Sprague grew tired of the Mary Campaign but stayed with it because it was successful. "We established an identity with those ads," she says. "It did give us a look."

Learning a New Market

Sprague decided to expand out of the New York market. In November 1982, she opened a unit in north Bethesda, Maryland, and in December 1983, another in Fairfax, Virginia. Both units are in shopping malls, catering to many Washington, D.C. commuters.

"We discovered many things that made us rethink our market direction," Sprague says. "The Mary Campaign had no validity in that market. They didn't want to be dressed by her. They didn't want to look like her. They just didn't care about her."

Victory was no longer dealing with the shopper off the streets of New York who wanted service, speed, quality, and wanted it yesterday. The service-oriented approach worked perfectly for the hurried New Yorker who stopped in during a lunch break, or on the way home. But in Fairfax and Bethesda Sprague encountered an unknown beast—the mall market. Not only did the Mary Campaign go nowhere, but advertisements in *The Washington Post* and *The Washingtonian* magazine fell flat. The personal, no self-service approach that worked in Manhattan wasn't for the typical mall shopper who was strolling along, browsing, and probably avoiding an approach by a friendly salesperson.

"We found that the things that worked were things we would never think of doing in New York. Large signage. Signs with messages like 'Buy a French cuff shirt and get a pair of cufflinks free' brought them in the door." Both stores had breakeven years in 1984, and were up 23 percent over 1983. "Both will be profitable in 1985," Sprague says.

Meeting Market Demands

While Victory took a hiatus from the Mary Campaign in the fall of 1984 ("Our regular customers complained when I stopped appearing."), Victory shirts continues to use print media for effective advertising of its New York stores. A women's line has been introduced into the inventory. At first the women's shirt had the classic male look, but Sprague sees the styles altering a bit as women become more secure in the workforce. "They'll wear a softer look," Sprague observes, noting that women's shirts now account for about 36 percent of total sales. She'd like to get that up to around 40 percent of gross sales.

As she puts out her cigarette and walks to the main sales area, she reminds me, "Brooks Brothers is right across the street. My staff and I are constantly running across the street to check out their prices. This will never be a passive investment for me."

MARKETING MESSAGES

Think Win-Win. Risks come with the entrepreneurial turf. So do mistakes. Make up your mind you are going to learn—and succeed by encountering both.

Behind the product there's you. The Mary Campaign was a winner because it gave customers the feeling that a real live person stood behind the product. It made her stand out in the crowd.

Say it again, and again, and again. Repetition is a key in building market recognition. Mary Sprague ran ads every ten days in *The Wall Street Journal*—not very frequently, but consistently. The effect was almost magical.

The Panic Factor. Don't let success throw you. When things start to roll, entrepreneurs sometimes panic and think they're getting into uncomfortably deep water. Have faith. Outside "experts" didn't make you, and they probably can't match the instincts that built your business in the first place. Trust yourself.

Chapter Fifteen

Special Events: "Canoecopia?" Sure I Can

In one weekend in March, Gordy Sussman, owner of the Madison, Wisconsin, canoe shop called "Rutabaga," makes almost 20 percent of his yearly gross sales. The reason is "Canoecopia," a two-day special canoe exposition Sussman has organized every year since 1978.

Gordy Sussman is a bearded man, somewhere in his thirties. Unkempt hair, blue ragwool sweater, Levis cords. Well-broken-in deck shoes. The store is hopping. "Canoecopia 85" is only about two weeks away, and Sussman is in the midst of preparations.

His office is an interesting study of Sussman's personality. An empty Mountain Dew bottle sits on his desk. An A&W root beer empty lies under his desk chair. Rubber-banded canceled checks and bill stubs are stacked all over the office. A straw cowboy hat with an "All The Way With LBJ" band sits on top of an old filing cabinet. Shadeless lamps complement an assortment of unplugged clock radios. An IBM typewriter, well over 20-years-old, sits on a stand behind him. Disciplined exuberance.

In 1984, on a Saturday and Sunday, at the Forum in Madison, around 9,700 people attended his free exposition. Sussman sold 207 canoes—$160,000 in gross sales for the two days.

Not bad for a business which had its beginnings in the basement of a Madison apartment in 1976. And not bad for a guy who landed in Madison by mistake in the first place.

"I was hitchhiking to Colorado," Sussman remembers in the loft office space in back of Rutabaga's South Park Street retail-store. "I was hitchhiking to Colorado, and in Youngstown, Ohio, I went north on route 90 instead of south on 80."

Sussman graduated from the University of Wisconsin in 1974. While a student there, he raced kayak, and there began what were to be the rudiments of Rutabaga. "I'd buy a half dozen paddles and sell five, keep one," he recalls. The five he sold would more than pay for the one he kept.

Staging a Full-Scale Exposition

"We've been doing "Canoecopia" since 1978 or so," Sussman says. "We started advertising it as 'Meet the Folks Who Build the Boats.' In 1982, we decided to go full throttle and have it at the Forum. We spend about $15,000-a-year advertising it nationally in *Canoe* magazine, and regionally in different outdoor and environment magazines.

"The first year at 5:30 in the morning I felt we had everything in line. But the weather wouldn't cooperate. I kept humming that old song, 'A Man Should Never Gamble More Than He Can Stand To Lose.'"

In spite of the weather and Sussman's ominous humming, the first year at the Forum 4,200 people showed up. In 1983, 8,000 showed up. In 1984, it was 9,700, and Sussman expects more than 10,000 in 1985.

"Canoecopia" has also helped in-store sales for Rutabaga. "By being out there with seminars and clinics, we're giving them a lot of feedback. We don't ever go out and sell the canoe. We go out and sell the sport."

Sussman organizes "Canoecopia" himself. Foremost in his mind is that it be valuable to his customers. "I gotta look at why the thing is there," he says. "The sales part has to be subjugated to the education part.

"It's like Oriental philosophy, I guess," he says, smiling. "I never really noticed that... son-of-a-gun. To get what you want you have to know what you want, but you can't go out and get it. To have the biggest canoe sale, you have to have the biggest exposition. It's not just a semantic difference. I'm not selling canoes—I'm selling the enhancement, the enjoyment of them.

"If I can tell people how to come to this building on a particular day and learn how to enjoy themselves, learn quite a bit, enhance their feeling toward canoes, then they're going to buy for the right reason because the perceived need is going to be created.

"I don't like the idea of buffaloing somebody to get them to buy something—you know 'Buy now and get the screen doors free.'"

The phone rings. Sussman talks, gets up and shouts out to his sales staff on the floor, "How about unloading boats at 8 o'clock tomorrow morning?" Several of them shout back, "Sure." "You have no brains, I can't believe it," Sussman shouts down. He returns to the phone call.

Staging special events is an excellent marketing tool that many smaller businesses find useful. Not all share Sussman's philosophical outlook on them, however. Some merely see it as a way to promote their products, clean their inventories, or increase sales during off-peak times. Underlying Sussman's Barthian-like refusal to name directly that which he is seeking, are these same fundamental motives.

Promoting Products, Cleaning Inventory, and Increasing Sales in Off-Peak Times

Pageants, events—whatever the entrepreneur chooses to call them—pay off. For example, Gary Scaife, director of marketing for Natural Choice Industries, Inc., Westlake, California, says that in conjunction with his Pink Panther and Sons juice products line his company cosponsors the "California Beach Girl Beauty Pageant." From May until August, contests are held up and down the coast of California. A final pageant is held in November at Universal Studios, the Pink Panther's home turf. The pageant is titled "Stay In The Pink," playing on the product name. "We get a lot of coverage on something like that," Scaife tells me. "We look to this type of promotion to return between $8 and $10 for every advertising dollar we spend."

Twice a year, Victory Shirt Company, Inc., Manhattan, runs a special irregular sale. "Because we make our own shirts, if anything's wrong with them, we're stuck with them," says Mary Sprague, president and owner of Victory. "To get rid of them we stamp them 'irregular' and mark them 50 percent off for a final sale. We used to advertise it. We no longer do. We only telemarket it to regular customers. We do it in January and July, typically slow months for us. It keeps our inventory clean."

When Sprague got to her Madison Avenue shop at 7:30 on the morning of the January 1985 sale, customers were already beginning to line up outside the store. By 9 o'clock, the line had turned the corner and was running down 44th Street. The sale is run at Victory's Madison Avenue and Maiden Lane locations. "We probably did about $45,000 in one day at the two stores," Sprague boasts.

Organizing the Event

When Gordy Sussman gets off the phone, we return to our discussion of "Canoecopia," for which he's booked the Forum on the same date in March through 1990.

"The Forum is pretty much booked for eternity," Sussman says. "We weasled a date out of them a few years ago. It costs us around $2,400 dollars to rent the space for two days. We rent some warehouse space as well.

"There's a $2 county parking charge. Beyond that it's free to the public. There's no charge for manufacturers to exhibit. In 1985 we'll have nine boat manufacturers, four sailboat manufacturers, three dozen accessory and clothing manufacturers, and a dozen public service booths. The public service booths are 10′ x 10′. A manufacturer or canoe company will get 30′ x 80′—whatever it takes to allow people to move around. There's also a 400-seat auditorium."

While Rutabaga has only four full-time employees, more than 100 people help out by working at "Canoecopia."

"My friends help out and work," Sussman says. "They get a 'Canoecopia' tee-shirt and we put on a big dinner on Saturday night at 'Canoecopia' for them."

Doing the Best for the Customer

Sussman thinks "Canoecopia" is an excellent way not only to sell canoes, but to serve his customers. "There's a period of anxiety in canoe sales," he says. "Customers have to make intelligent decisions rather than reflex decisions. If you handle it right you can put them at ease and sell them what they need. Once somebody is served well, they're going to bring friends in.

"With retail you cannot concern yourself only with profit and closing the sale, but with doing the best you can for the consumer. Your profit should not be the main concern.

"We give the customer a buy-back guarantee. Within two years if they don't like the boat, we'll give them a minimum of two-thirds back towards the cost of another boat. None of this has to do with success or profitability. It has to do with sleeping easily at night.

"Canoeing is great recreation. During the peak season, I will have people come in just to jaw about it. The whole idea is if you get somebody enthused, you're doing it properly. The primary business of Rutabaga is to be the best canoe shop in the country."

That said, it's clear Sussman is still concerned with the bottom line on Rutabaga's financial statement. "The whole thing about entrepreneurs," he philosophizes, "is their attitude toward money. If money's perceived as a means, then the person's an entrepreneur. Money is nice the same way as getting a gold star on a paper in the second grade was nice—positive reinforcement. The only way I really have of telling I'm doing well is the bottom line. If my employees and customers are happy and remain friends, that's a good measure of success. But it's subjective."

Several months later, I talk with Sussman about how "Canoecopia 85" fared. He tells me that in two days he sold 240 boats and grossed a little over $250,000. The company also just opened another store in Milwaukee. Since the next date at the Forum in 1986 falls on Easter, Sussman is toying with the idea of having "Canoecopia" at the Milwaukee State Fair Grounds, and alternating it back and forth every year.

Not bad prospects for Sussman, who began his canoe business humbly enough by selling kayak paddles and then investing $400 and moving to an old Bandit gas station a few blocks down from his current Madison store. The gas station no longer exists. Sussman's canoe business, however, continues to paddle on, stronger with each new stroke.

MARKETING MESSAGES

In marketing, the play's the thing. Create an event, a need. Special sales give you a chance to move goods creatively. The market thinks the sales event is *the* event of this or any other season.

"PPCII"—It stands for Promoting Products, Cleaning Inventories, Increasing off-peak sales. These are the call letters of special sales marketing. If the sale is special enough, the potential is enormous.

Chapter Sixteen

Seminars as a Lure

Somewhere a group of businesspeople sit listening. There may be 75 people, perhaps as many as 150. They've come to hear about smoking in the work place, from a health, legal, and cost-to-business standpoint.

"Nine states [Hawaii, Maine, New Jersey, Colorado, Connecticut, Minnesota, Montana, Nebraska, and Utah] specifically regulate smoking in the private sector workplace, and all but 14 states have restrictions on smoking in the private sector," Robert A. Rosner, Dr. William Weis, and attorney Timothy Lowenberg wrote in their op-ed piece in *The Washington Post* in the spring of 1985. They also wrote about the results of employee smoking research conducted at Weyerhauser, a major forest products company. Weyerhauser estimated that smoking costs at corporate headquarters alone were running $4.9 million-a-year. The article continued:

"By applying published research on work-site smoking costs to its facilities, Weyerhauser pinpointed the following hidden costs of smoking at work:

"*Insurance premiums: Male heavy smokers use the health care system, particularly hospitals, 50 percent more than nonsmokers. Reducing the number of smokers could reduce corporate health care coverage premiums $394,457.

"*Absenteeism: Smokers average 50 percent more absences than nonsmokers.

"*Productivity: Smokers waste 30 minutes-a-day in the smoking ritual. This results in a collective annual time loss of 44-man-years.

"*Mortality: During their [sic] working lifetime, a smoker is 70 percent more likely to die than a nonsmoker."

In April 1984, Rosner, Weis, and Lowenberg formed a health/management consulting service based in Seattle, Washington, called, appropriately enough, Rosner, Weis & Lowenberg, Inc. (RW&L). Lowenberg brought legal expertise to the group. He's a partner in the Tacoma, Washington, law firm of Schweinler, Lowenberg & Lopez, as well as adjunct professor of law at the University of Puget Sound School of Law.

Weis brings the numbers expertise. He's the chairman of the accounting department at Albers School of Business at Seattle University. And Rosner, president of RW&L brings the public relations expertise. Rosner worked on a variety of consumer-oriented health projects in the Tacoma/Seattle area since his graduation with an occupational therapy major from the University of Puget Sound in 1980.

"Our goal is not to prohibit smoking or to be on a crusade against smoking," Rosner says early one morning in his office in Seattle. "We're simply helping companies determine what they should do about the smoking issue. A lot of people try to put us up as fanatics and crusaders, especially the Tobacco Institute. That's not what we're about at all."

RW&L was formed as a for-profit operation to help companies research the smoking issue and determine the implications it may have in terms of health and safety, legal liability, cost containment, and employee morale. "We help companies see their options and advise them how to follow through," says Rosner.

Seminars as an Information/Marketing Tool

To attract clients, which now number over 20 companies, the seminar is a chief information/marketing lure to draw interest to what RW&L has to offer. At $800-a-day plus expenses to run a workshop, or $100-an-hour for consultation, with a consultation taking anywhere from 5 or 10 to 100 hours, RW&L has grown slowly but steadily, establishing a good track record.

The reaction of some of its clients bears testimony. RW&L did a consulting job for CIGNA Healthplan of Arizona, Inc., in Phoenix. "I was there for three days, met with the upper management, middle management, and gave a presentation to the warehouse folks," says Rosner. "After all that scouting around, I met with the health promotion and personnel people about how to implement the plan.

"They said they wanted to have smoking banned by April 1 [1985]. They wanted to do it on their own, but not to reinvent the wheel. We were brought in as consultants. It was a situation where they had the troops to implement the policy, but they needed to establish the policy."

After his consultation, the coordinator of the health and fitness program at CIGNA Healthplan wrote Rosner:

"Implementation is going along very smoothly, even in the several departments where I had anticipated resistance. Administration has approved free smoking cessation classes in conjunction with free Nicorettes [nicotine-substitute chewing gum] for those employees who have made the decision to cut down or quit.... A number of employees have already quit or cut down substantially in anticipation of our April 1 date of implementation...."

RW&L may not be fanatics or crusaders, but, if Rosner is any example, the company certainly is obsessed with its mission. "The bottom line is that the tobacco companies have really been the only group arguing this issue. They've been doing a suicide run to keep the industry intact. My perception," Rosner says, "is that we're being viewed as experts and they're being viewed as carpetbaggers.

"It's in our interest that employees have a safe and healthy work environment. We're helping companies deal with that issue."

Finding Local Cosponsors

So Rosner will stand in front of businesspeople at a seminar in a downtown hotel giving them an idea of the implications of the smoking issue. RW&L never puts up the money for the seminars. The company is compensated for its time. Usually the seminar is cosponsored by local citizens and business groups, and a group like Smoke Enders, a division of Comprehensive Care.

"We try to find a group which has a lot of local credibility," Rosner explains. "The Chamber of Commerce sponsored one of the workshops in Seattle. We match the local credibility with an organization that has some financial interest in the workplace."

Refining the Message

RW&L averages about 100 businesspeople attending each of the seminars, and it's led to a lot of follow-up consulting business. But at first all the kinks weren't worked out.

"We really didn't have our materials together to do follow-up marketing," Rosner admits. "Quite frankly, we were a little antagonistic in our message at first. Now we are more aware of our message. We want to be proactive, not antagonistic. At each workshop we have more and more potential clients. We've gotten almost all of our clients via the workshop route."

RW&L runs its seminars at little financial risk, since it has cosponsors paying its fee. Other companies, such as Costello, Erdlen & Co., Inc., a human resource consulting firm, pay for their own seminars.

Hands-On Information

Costello, Erdlen & Co., Inc., has main offices in Quincy and Wellesley, Massachusetts, and is in the midst of building impressive headquarters in Westwood that will house two operations. Its success is due in large part to an aggressive marketing program based on seminars.

"We do about four seminars a quarter in New England and Chicago," says Jack Erdlen at his Wellesley office. "We try to provide a 'hands-on' basis, not from a theoretical viewpoint, but from the way it actually happens. We look to get anywhere from 12 to 20 people at these things.

"The seminars show we have expertise. It's a combination of a training and marketing tool for us. We just feel, hey, if you show up enough places, sooner or later you'll get your share, or continue to get your share."

Rosner says RW&L now has clients in Phoenix, southern California, Minnesota, Seattle, and Portland, Oregon. "We started the company with no money essentially," Rosner boasts. "Each of us put in $200."

The RW&L seminars are well-structured. They are two hours long. In the first ten minutes an overview of the issue is presented. The next ten minutes focus on health and safety. Then a half-hour on legal liability, followed by ten minutes of legislation, a half-hour on cost containment and benefits, and the remaining time on implementation. Questions in the two-hour time frame of the seminar come at the end. For about a half-hour, the three partners, who attend every seminar, will head to different parts of the room and take on questions.

Rosner tells me his approach at the seminars is no longer as "crusading" as it might have appeared in the beginning.

"I present the health issue at the seminars by saying, 'For those of you who expected to see black lungs, you're not going to see them. What I have for you is information.' I then describe the effects of carbon monoxide on the workplace and ask them, 'Is this the environment you want your employees to work in?'

"At the end of this part of the seminar, I have a room full of business executives whose eyes are pretty wide. I take the social, health, and safety issue and put it in a business context."

Enlightened Self-Interest

"We don't hide the fact that we're a for-profit company," says Rosner. "The operative term in my life is enlightened self-interest. As a company, I'm realizing that it's sometimes possible to do good in a community and also do well financially for myself."

RW&L is in the early stages of development, so the financial return is not overwhelming to-date. "We've taken this thing very slowly. Our two major goals now are to develop smoking policies at as many companies in the country as we can, and to deal with high visibility companies.

"We've been able to parlay the seminars into national exposure," says Rosner. "The three of us have very different styles, but they're complementary. We put on a pretty sophisticated dog-and-pony show."

MARKETING MESSAGES

Seminars inform your market. These show-your-wares information forums generate image, interest, and follow-up business.

The price is right. You can pay for your own seminar or find cosponsorship from civic and business groups. Either way, overhead is very low and cost-effective.

Chapter Seventeen

Public Relations: You Need What We Have

Thumbing through *Vanity Fair* for February 1985, you come upon a Valentine's Day fashion spread. David Byrne of the new wave rock group, "Talking Heads," is the object of a model's affection. If you notice the earrings the model's wearing on page 71 of the issue, the page on which Byrne wears the now famous too-big suit that he donned in the movie *Stop Making Sense*, you're noticing the result of a successful public relations effort launched by the earring designer herself, Barbara Vay.

Vay may live in North Arlington, New Jersey, a bedroom community that's 20 minutes outside of Manhattan, but she's strictly Bronx at the roots. She was born and raised in the Bronx and graduated in 1982 from the School of Graphic Arts in New York.

"It was really a fluke with *Vanity Fair*," Vay recalls in the living room of the North Arlington home where she lives and works. "I went there on a Friday afternoon. They had a shoot they were going to do the following day. The whole point is to keep getting publicity. I must have 200 pieces lent out. The longer they have the piece, the more shoots they can go out on, the more publicity."

Public relations, for many small businesses, is a crucial ingredient of getting a product or service implanted firmly in the minds of the potential market. Some, like Vay, are capable of handling their own public relations; others rely on outside public relations firms. In either case, a successful public relations campaign can pay off quite nicely.

Building an Event: Pushing the Product

Vay certainly pays plenty of attention to PR. "The past few months have been a whirlwind," she says. "I've really put myself into pushing my work. If you want anything, you have to get it yourself."

She is constantly buzzing. Even when she sits talking with me she plays with an earring, taps a foot, shifts in her seat. While her earrings are avant garde and large, "rough glamour," she likes to describe them, and she is a rather petite woman, she wears her own earrings and they seem a natural part of her outfit—oversized translucent white-framed glasses, a jeans jacket, red high-top boxing shoes, and black tight skipants.

Vay was actively promoting her calligraphy and collage work before she began "doing" jewelry in June 1984. The jewelry collection on the coffee table in her living room "evolved since October 1984." She only started showing her work in December 1984, but by the end of February 1985, her earrings had appeared in *Vanity Fair*, *Harper's Bazaar*, and on the ears of soap opera stars in "Ryan's Hope" and "As The World Turns." ABC purchased some of Vay's earrings to use on "Ryan's Hope." But "As The World Turns" borrowed them in exchange for giving her credit at the end of the show. When Vay's jewelry is used it is either purchased or will receive credit. It never goes unnoticed.

Vay's jewelry is also carried at Henri Bendel's store in New York City. "They're a hot specialty type store on 57th, just off Fifth Avenue," she says. Her earrings are also at Serendipity's at West 60th and Third Avenue.

Going From One Person to the Next

Vay works hard, but she's not too amazed at her success, which is built chiefly on her product but equally on her persistence. Her level of stamina is akin to a triathlete in an iron-man competition. "I just went around to the stores, magazines, and TV shows," says Vay. "I'd call up the station and go from one person to the next."

Of course, Vay must also find time to produce the actual jewelry she promotes. Being a 24-hour-a-day entrepreneur helps. She designs the jewelry outside of business hours when she could be promoting. While she may appear a bit manic, she's quite in control, and her work schedule is carefully planned out so that everything will get done.

"A lot of good artists don't know how to sell themselves," she says. "I'll call people 50 times in one day. It gets them to the point of thinking, 'Maybe she has something.' or 'I'll see her just to shut her up.' If it's the latter, the work usually sells itself."

Make Them Aware You Exist

Merrill Diamond, who with Gordon Hurwitz, owns the Brookline, Massachusetts-based real estate developer, Parencorp, also believes his product can sell itself, but a little nudging doesn't hurt. He confides that the day *Boston* magazine came out listing him and Hurwitz as two of the "85 Faces To Watch in 85," he was in negotiation on a piece of property when a lawyer told him, "Look, you don't get in *Boston* magazine by being stupid."

Stupid, no. A little pushy, maybe. "We decided we should be one of the 85 in 85," Diamond says. So the company asked its public relations firm to put together a packet and send it to the editor who was handling the "Faces To Watch" special.

"We made them aware we existed," says Diamond, realizing that the chances were just as likely that the packet of PR material could have ended up in the trash. "The good things that have happened to us, we made happen. It's taking something that was nothing and turning it into something."

Stephen Garber, owner of the London Wine Company, which is just down the street from Merrill Diamond's office in Brookline, also understands the importance of carefully placed public relations. He donated some money to the local public radio station, in exchange for which, every night at 5:30, Stephen Garber and the London Wine Company get a mention as making a portion of the evening's "All Things Considered" broadcast possible.

"I found underwriting public radio very helpful," Garber says. "Everybody goes out of their way to tell me how appreciative they are. It's just a message, once a night, five-nights-a-week, 52-weeks-a-year at 5:30," he adds with a smile, "when 99 percent of their listening population will hear it."

Garber knows that by being on National Public Radio, London Wine comes off with a very sophisticated image. He also knows that when people happen upon his store in the Coolidge Corner area of Brookline, they might recall the name they hear mentioned on radio night after night. Garber likes the fact that people perceive him and his shop as making a half-hour of "All Things Considered" possible.

Tell Everyone About It

Barbara Vay is always on duty when it comes to doing her own public relations. Since she wears earrings from the collection she's designed, and since they are fairly unusual, she will often be stopped on the street or in a store and asked about the earrings she's wearing. "When I'm out and people ask me where I got my earrings, I say, 'These? Oh, Barbara Vay designed them.'" She rarely tells the person that she is Barbara Vay, but chooses instead to plant the notion that they should already be familiar with Barbara Vay's work. If they're not, she'll tell them how to get a pair.

Joan Schneider, owner of a public relations firm in Brookline, Massachusetts, Schneider & Associates, gives us the following definition of PR:

"Public relations is taking something, even if it's intrinsically boring, and making it fabulously interesting and telling everybody about it."

Her basic philosophy about her own approach to business which she passes on to her clients, and which seems to have roots in her experience with the 1970's self awareness seminars, "est," is that, "if you really think you can do something, even if others thought you couldn't, it's important to do it."

Target the PR Pitch

Vay knows how to selectively target her pitch. "I met with the buyer of Neiman Marcus' Dallas store because the New York City buyer is too conservative," she explains.

Vay's earrings are far from conservative. They stem from her collage work. "Shapes. I use cork, clay, papier mache, sealing wax, wire. I'm very excited about the new collage pieces."

To an untrained eye, many of the earrings look like they're in the shape of Africa or other large land masses you think you should be able to recognize. "I don't intend the shapes to look like anything," Vay insists. "Everybody thinks they look like land masses. What I like about my work is the roughness of the edges. Kind of a rough glamour. All of my work has an abstract, sculptural quality, an ugly glamour."

To keep up with possible publicity avenues, Vay buys hundreds of magazines. "All the magazines have to have jewelry for their layouts," she explains. "Soap operas need costuming. Choosing publicity outlets in itself is pretty easy." Although she doesn't admit it, Vay probably is as up-to-date as anyone can be on the soap opera plot lines, as well as magazine strengths and weaknesses.

Her PR push has been very effective, but Vay is not satisfied. Nervously, she says, "I'm never happy. I mean I'm happy, but I'm not *happy*. You know what I mean?"

"People want to talk with me now," she says. "I have a product. It's difficult because art is the product, but I have a product to show. I'm also developing a distinctive 'look.' People have told me my works look like me. I even do things now and they say, 'Oh, that's so Barbara Vay.' I just want to keep growing. I have developed a style that I really want to push."

Through persistent pushing, Vay has managed very early in her business career to gain publicity that is usually very difficult to find. Like Joan Schneider, Barbara Vay shares the belief that if you really think you can do something, even if others think you can't, "it's important to do it."

MARKETING MESSAGES

Do good and tell about it. There is always a "little nudging factor" in PR. You have a good product or service, so tell the media, tell the market, tell everyone who will listen. Keep the message coming.

The "P" in PR stands for persistence. Persistence is the operative word. One of the main objects of PR is to keep getting more of it. So firmly implant your product or service in the collective mind of the market and keep ringing the bells.

Sell yourself and sell hard. Successful entrepreneurs know the value of selling themselves. CEO's such as Robert Brennan of First Jersey Securities, Lee Iacocca of Chrysler, and Frank Perdue of chicken fame have learned—profitably—that the market wants to know who's minding the store.

Chapter Eighteen

Television Advertising: Beyond the Rest

A balding, bearded man talks to the camera. He's working at his jeweler's bench. There's a safe in the background, and someone, someplace is tinkling the piano ivories like a lounge pianist vamping between numbers. "I'm going to use a four letter word on television," the conservative-looking jeweler tells his audience. Then he holds up a sign reading "SALE" and explains that Condon's Jewelers never runs sales because their prices are already so reasonable. Condon's doesn't artificially inflate prices, so it can cut them later for a sale. The piece ends with the gentleman jeweler staring us down and announcing, "Condon's—Beyond the rest."

While many people viewing these ad spots, which were filmed in 1982, think that the man talking is Jerry Condon, he is not. His name is Reed Farrell, an actor out of Chicago who was cast by the Milwaukee-based Jim Hughes Advertising, Condon's ad agency. In fact, when Farrell appeared in a print ad in *The Wall Street Journal* recently for a different product, many readers who knew the Condon's ads thought Jerry Condon was plugging products in the *Journal.*

Condon's is a Madison, Wisconsin, jewelry store that's been around since 1959, when the first store opened downtown. By the end of 1984, it had five stores and annual sales of around $4.25 million, according to Edward Amsdell, Condon's general manager.

Choosing the Right Ad Agency

In 1978, Jerry Condon recognized that his advertising, which was being produced chiefly by Channel 15, Madison's NBC affiliate, had become stagnant. He sought out an advertising agency that could set him out apart from the rest. Enter Jim Hughes.

"Before Hughes, we were basically sticking our stuff on channels 15 and 27," Condon says as we sit with Jim Hughes and Ed Amsdell in a conference room full of smoke, Condon's jewelers posterboards, and some videotape equipment.

Hughes, who has driven down from Milwaukee during a freak snowstorm, has managed to get the video equipment here, but the person who was supposed to be delivering the tape of advertisements is stuck somewhere in the snow.

Looking for Real Breakthroughs

"We're a consumer agency," Hughes says of his Milwaukee-based advertising firm. "We have two people who do nothing but look at various media, week in and week out. We started to develop something with Jerry that would really be a breakthrough, just to take Jerry out of the mainstream."

Prior to running its series of balding jeweler ads, Condon's had run an ad which caused a bit of a stir in the Madison market. The ad, as described by various local luminaries, featured a woman swimming in a pool apparently dressed only in jewelry. Many people were apparently appalled that Condon would run such an ad, and it was later pulled, to be followed by the much more conservative balding jeweler ads. However controversial that first ad was, it certainly did start to make Condon's stand out.

When his agency began to develop the balding jeweler series, Hughes remembers "I talked to the store managers and got a lot of good input from them. We took a look at the marketplace and saw every other outlet was constantly in a sales posture. At one of our major meetings, we said 'Let's flount never having sales.' It was different posture that surprised everyone. We come on saying our everyday sales were low enough."

The shift to a balding, conservative looking actor as the spokesperson for Condon's was also important to the marketing strategy. "We went into a long casting process to find him," says Hughes. "We looked at at least 15 different acting talents."

Marketing to an Intelligent Audience

Condon also recognized that he was marketing to an intelligent audience which, in the late 1970s, realized there might be more bang for the jewelry buck by taking advantage of the low-priced mass merchants.

"Jerry saw it coming," says Hughes. "That's when we decided to position Condon more nose-to-nose with the retailers."

After the original series of ads, which always ended with Reed Farrell reading the tag line, "Condon's, beyond the rest," Hughes and Condon's began to take on the retailer more directly. "In our series we ran in the fourth quarter of 1984," recalls Hughes, "we decided to go against the mass retailers. We were really the only ones doing anything different in advertising."

Two of the ads poked not-so-veiled fun at the competence of department store clerks. The first had the balding jeweler ask, "Would you really like to send a jewelry gift that came from the same store that sold you this tie?" And then he proceeds to hold up the ugliest tie you could imagine. He doesn't answer his own questions, but you're supposed to be sitting home saying, "Of course I wouldn't." The ad continues, "Fair prices. People behind the counter who know what they're doing."

The next head-on department store critique asked, "Would you feel comfortable buying a fine watch like this from a department store clerk who might have spent last week selling shoes?"

Of course not. The ad continues: "Do it right. Buy from a full-time jewelry store." Both ads end with the same "Condon's, beyond the rest," that the earlier ads ended with.

Taking on the Competition

But Condon's and Hughes didn't stop here. Next they developed a concept they called "bottom line pricing" in their ads. This time they weren't necessarily taking on department stores, but aimed instead at chain jewelry store and discount jewelry store competition.

"All other retail jewelers in the business are doing what the competition is doing," says Hughes. "Everybody's overpricing and then having 50 percent sales. We decided at that point to sell jewelry and not a lot of hot air. Let's tell them the market value and then tell them our price. In the window of our stores, we give the market value and the bottom line price.

"It's been extremely effective. There's been a 15-to-20 percent increase in sales every month since we introduced it. One of the things we've found is that when they come into the stores they're asking for the bottom line price."

Adds, Condon: "We're not a discount store. We price it right to start with. In the retail industry, stores usually must get three times the cost or they will not sell it. We don't operate that way. They have to do it so they can have those big sales."

So bottom line pricing was worked into the balding jeweler ads. In fact, the first of these ads begins with a montage of sales pitches and balloons and streamers that typically plague sales ads, only to have a balloon popped by Farrell announcing that those sales are only so much hot air. "At Condon's we start our prices where the competitors end up," announces Farrell. The ad ends with the usual "Condon's, beyond the rest," tag, just in case you already didn't realize they stood out from the crowd.

The Message Sinks In

The most recent bottom line pricing ad is a real breakthrough as far as Hughes is concerned because it was shot on location with 35-millimeter film, rather than the usual videotape. "The consumer can see it. If you want to do something that'll knock their socks off, you use 35-millimeter. We shot it on location at Milwaukee's Commission Row."

In the piece, Farrell, in tweedy dress, uses the analogy of apples and oranges to talk about bottom line pricing and the sales other stores stage. You guessed it—the ad shows a box of fresh apples and a box of fresh oranges. "Don't let the illusion of a sale take a bite out of your jewelry dollar," the tweed-capped jeweler tells us, as he bites into his apple and walks off screen. Not only is this ad different because it uses 35-millimeter, but it's also the first time without the use of the delightful little piano tinkling in the background. More importantly it does not close with the tag, "Condon's, beyond the rest." The ad simply ends with the sound of an apple crunching.

This is an important step. It seems that after six years of repositioning Condon's, Jerry Condon and Hughes are comfortable that the market realizes that Condon's jewelry stores are so obviously different that they no longer have to remind the viewers about it.

The Impact of the TV Campaign

The impact of the advertising Condon's is running, which costs about 5 to 5.5 percent of its gross sales every year, is quite broad in the market. Hughes runs through his most recent breakdown of advertising data and explains: "In an average week we'll be on television 35 times. Our gross ratings points are 194, which means that we reach 72.9 percent of the viewers with a frequency of 3 times-a-week. The actual reach is 193,400. By the end of the schedule we're up to 85 percent, 45.5 times over the course of a year, which means that 45.5 times over the year we'll reach 85.5 percent of our demographic—the 18-to-49-year-olds.

"For anybody who has a market position and a reputation like Jerry, I really think the answer is to keep doing what you're doing. It doesn't take much to be outstanding. There's a lot of 'dreck' out there that will go by the wayside."

Agency/Client Relationship

The importance of developing a good relationship with an ad agency or with the production house which is producing ads is tantamount to success. "From my standpoint," Hughes tells me later as we drive to the East Towne Mall so I can have a look at Condon's, "we're able to do what we can do because Jerry put us on the team. There are no secrets. We'll hear about all the problems. For me an agency should be treated like an accountant, lawyer, or anybody else. It's nice to work with someone like Jerry who puts you on the team."

In the East Towne Mall, the Condon's store is on one of the busier corners, in front of one of the major fountains. There's a boat show going on so there's a crowd here on this Monday afternoon. In the display window of the store are little black markers that list the market value next to the bottom line price of the displayed items. On the items displayed, the bottom line prices seem to be about 20 percent less than the market value.

Inside the store on the counter is a bowl of Condon's Jewelers matches, just under a sign which reads, "No smoking per order of the Fire Chief."

Consistent Image

You can catch a bus from in front of the East Towne Mall which will let you off right in front of Condon's store in the Capitol Square area of town. Right across from the Capitol Square store is the state capitol building which looms over everything in the area. There are no competing jewelry stores on this block of East Mifflin Street. While the outside street traffic certainly differs from that at the East Towne Mall, when you walk inside you could just as easily be in any of the Condon's jewelry stores.

Says Hughes: "There's a real consistency from store-to-store. We hope there's a feel of professionalism, consistent service. A Condon's is a Condon's."

But Hughes draws the line short of considering Condon's jewelry stores to be a slickly packaged chain. He'd rather think that as a result of Condon's working with Jim Hughes Advertising, they are better positioned than they are packaged.

"We'll maintain the bottom line pricing approach and probably move back into a little more product sell," Hughes explains. "We've been doing the bottom line pricing for two years now, so we can maintain it and probably go back into the product sell. We can now say words like 'bottom line pricing' and just about everybody will know what we mean."

Hughes can also leave out tags like "Condon's, beyond the rest," because just about everybody in the market, they'd like to believe, knows it already. The teamwork between Condon's and Hughes resulted in a big score with market positioning that pays off in increased sales.

Marketing Messages

Treat your TV audience with respect. If you aim low, you'll miss the market. Make your ad appeal to intelligent perceptions.

Make the ad-makers a part of your team. You've hired professionals to get your message across, so fill them in on what you're trying to sell and what selling attempts—good or bad—you've made in the past. Let the ad executives get to know you, your product, and your sales personnel.

If it's not broken, don't fix it. If you're into a successful ad campaign, stay with it. You may vary it a little, make improvements, but know what is working and why. Set yourself apart from the crowd. Position yourself through your ads as *the* place for whatever it is you are marketing.

Chapter Nineteen

Direct Mail: Taking it to the Street

Direct mail, once the junkyard dog of marketing, has become one of the more well-respected avenues of getting the product pitch to the marketplace. Everything can be sold through direct mail these days. Hardly a day goes by when this fact is not driven home emphatically as you sort through your day's mail.

Almost any category of buyers from shipbuilders to screw machine part users is available in list form for the marketer to rent and try to hit. Karen Kukish Loh, marketing manager for Bankers Publishing Company in Boston, which markets its books solely through the mails, says, "We'll probably drop 850,000 pieces in 1985. That's about a 30 percent increase over 1984." With under 30 titles on its list, Bankers is relatively small. Imagine the volume of mail sent out by Time-Life Books, or Prentice-Hall.

The Marketable Life of a Product

"I try to pay a lot of attention to the marketable life of a product," Loh says, "and put as many pieces in the mail as profitability can stand."

Bankers mainstay book is their *Encyclopedia of Banking and Finance*. The eighth edition came out in 1983. "We started promoting the Encyclopedia in August of 1983," Loh recalls. "We've put around 193,000 pieces in the mail since then. We average anywhere from a .5 percent direct response [five orders for every thousand direct mail advertising pieces mailed] to a .9 percent [nine orders for every thousand pieces mailed]. I needed about .55 percent to break even on my mailing to recover costs. It's reaching the point where I can't put too many more pieces in the mail. The response rates are getting lower. Each time you go out to the same list, you've got to figure you'll get a 15-to-20 percent lower response on that list."

Bankers' *Commercial Loan Officer's Handbook* (CLOH) came out in October 1984, but Loh began a prepublication direct mail campaign the previous month to shore up reader interest.

"I did a prepublication mailing of a little more then 10,000 pieces. It was just a one-page letter and a card, less elaborate than our full-fledged mailing. We were just trying to hit our prime prospects. We got a 2.5 percent response to that. In October, after prepublication, we put 12,000 pieces in the mail, and went back in January with almost 13,000 pieces. I'm getting about a 2 percent response for this particular book."

For CLOH, which sells for $42.50, Bankers needed a .6 percent response for breakeven. Loh says Bankers will promote a new book four times in its first year. With something like CLOH, that probably means putting something like 50,000 pieces in the mail.

"I keep track of what's going on, not only in terms of direct response, but also in what percentage of a book's income marketing is taking up," she says. "That way I won't prematurely cut off the marketing life of a book. When I see marketing costs are eating up 30-to-33 percent of the book's sales, that's when I'll cut back."

Using Direct Mail as a Supplement

For companies like Bankers, direct mail is the lifeblood. But for the entrepreneur who uses other primary means of selling a product or service, direct mail can serve very well as an adjunct. For example, Stephen Garber of London Wine Company used sophisticated direct mail software to target upscale clients to market particular wines. Sales jumped as much as 50 percent.

Others find similar results, with or without the software. Bill's Florist in Boonton, New Jersey, dropped its first direct mail in November 1983, attempting to add a little life to holiday sales. "We took a flier and had sketches done up," says Dennis Goldenberg, who owns Bill's Florist with his father, Herb. "We saw a 48 percent increase over last year in holiday business that first holiday. We could track it because people would call up and order the arrangements by number right off the flier.

"Very few florists do their own direct marketing," Dennis says, implying that many prefer to use the standard FTD mailing pieces that are made available to them. "We mail to everybody on the taxpayer list in Boonton, Mountain Lakes, Boonton Township, plus 1,400 or 1,500 people outside of that." This past Valentine's Day, Bill's Florist, which ran another of its own direct mail campaigns, saw sales rise 33 percent over the previous year.

To make life simple for its salespeople and to reduce costs, Bill's limited the offerings on its direct mail pieces to two FTD nationwide advertised specials (the Merlin Olsen bouquets), plus six of its own designs. Sales continue to climb.

Using Riders on Mailing Pieces

While Bankers Publishing doesn't focus on the same type of multiple selection offerings that Bill's Florist uses so well, the company finds that riders for other products on an ad piece can be successful. "Riders on our ads for other books pull between 15 and 30 percent of the total books ordered for that campaign," says Loh. "For example, if I got 100 orders off of the CLOH direct mail piece, 70 will be for CLOH, and 30 of them are spread out among the riders. We started to use riders to increase the profitability of the piece that had been mailed seven or eight times to the same person."

Tracking the Untrackable: "White Mail"

While Loh is generally pleased with the direct response to the books, she's surprised at how well "white mail" sometimes called "drift mail"—orders that come in separate from any ad pieces—is doing.

"When there's a lot of drift mail coming in, I know the book's doing better than I thought it would. It means it's been well received. During the second six months a book is on the market, if 40-to-50 percent of the orders are coming in from drift mail, that's good. It means I'm marketing a lot and the market is responding well."

Some businesses expect white mail to follow from their direct mail campaigns. Palay Displays Industries, Inc., a retail clothing store display supplier in Grand Forks, North Dakota, is one such company. "In our business we don't rely on one-time purchases, but on an ongoing business relationship," Howard Palay tells me. So when the firm sends out a catalog or a direct mail piece, it expects the mailing to pull for some time.

The biggest mailing Palay Displays has done to-date came in April 1984, when 12,000 of its 39th anniversary catalogs were mailed. "The whole thing cost us probably $6,000 for printing, postage, names, and everything," Palay says. By February of the following year, the company gained at least 250 new accounts in 12 states. Not all are attributable to the mailing, of course, but the exposure didn't hurt.

"That was the first mailing of that type we'd ever done. Prior to that, we'd just send to existing accounts," Palay says. "We'd sometimes get phone books from nine of the states and pick out stores' names. 1984 was the first major direct mail attempt."

Refining the Campaign

As a result of the success with its first mailing, Palay Displays developed its own lists and now plans a mailing every quarter. "We've put together our own computer lists of sporting goods associations, women's ready-to-wear, western wear lists for Colorado and Montana," Palay explains. "We also bought a big list for sporting goods in 12 states. Once a year, we'll have a really big mailing to push for new accounts. Then three smaller mailings."

Profit in Direct Mail

At Bankers, Loh looks for anywhere from 25-to-35 percent of a gross profit on a mailing, which covers all costs but overhead. "I mail until there's no gross profit," she says.

In the beginning of 1985, Bankers Publishing spread its wings and began to market its first subscription product, a newsletter geared toward bankers which focuses on lending to small and middle-market companies. The subscription product presents new direct mail marketing challenges.

"The differences in marketing subscription products is not only in how you choose lists, but most of all in how you analyze the profitability of marketing. You need to figure out a way to quantify the additional income you're going to get from subscriber renewals," says Loh. "The newsletter was a real technical learning experience for me because it was more involved mathematically in conducting a breakeven for a particular list.

"Once we did our market test and had a real response rate to a real product, I sat down and did a forecast to see if I could stand a 20 percent decrease on each mailing and still end up with a profit after two years. I would be very happy with an active circulation of over 2,000 at the end of two years. That's a very small circulation even for a banking publication, but the banking market is exploding with new publications. We're facing some serious competition right now."

Bankers is dealing with a relatively small total market universe; Loh ballparks it at 220,000. Because of this, she is limited in how much testing of various packages she can do to see which ones pull best. The small numbers might skew the results and her ultimate marketing decision.

"I don't have the opportunity to do a lot of head-to-head testing for package and products," she says. "We do a lot more shooting in the dark than a professional publisher with a universe of a million does. Sometimes it's hard to come up with enough lists to split head-to-head and have significant results."

When she's putting together a direct mail package for one of Bankers book products, Loh relies on input from author, editor, and on what she perceives to be the market needs. But a good part of it comes from seat-of-the-pants experience. "You send it out and see if the response you get is anywhere near the response you want. So far we've been pretty successful."

With growing competition in the banking books market, Loh realizes how important it is to spend marketing dollars judiciously. Bankers, which has sales between $750,000 and $1 million annually, can't afford to throw away good money after bad on marketing failures. "We just can't keep producing products out there," says Loh. "We have to make sure they're being marketed properly and profitably. It's a matter of deciding what's the best place to spend our resources."

Marketing Messages

Mail until they're not buying it anymore. The beauty of direct mail is that you get hard, trackable results.

Call a dog a dog. If a particular mailing list bombs, get rid of it. But if all the lists you mail don't work, perhaps the problem lies in your product.

Mailing lists pinpoint the market. Lists are available for just about any market you can think of, thus the entrepreneur can tailor the pitch. Direct mail also gives you an opportunity to test prices and product offerings.

Maxim Five

The Open-Throttle Theory

Use All Your Tools and Talents. Hit the Market With Everything You've Got.

More and more, the public is beginning to perceive correctly that more than selling goes into the marketing process. By now you've seen product development, market research, quality control, targeting, product differentiation, and other aspects that go into successful marketing. Obviously, marketing involves a lot more than selling.

Hitting the market—making sure your product is there so the public can buy it. That's the critical link in the marketing chain.

In the following chapters, you'll meet many businesspeople who use different methods to get their products to market. You'll meet the people of PRO-ED, an educational publishing house in Austin, Texas, which uses one large catalog as its primary means of selling more than 600 titles focusing on special education and testing. You'll see how a food manufacturer has gotten itself off of the specialty food shelf at the grocery store and into the mainstream, right next to the big name noodle and rice products. You'll learn how a kite manufacturer in Marblehead, Massachusetts, learned to limit its selection so distribution wouldn't become bogged down during the peak kite-buying season. And you'll peek a bit into the future as a small clothing store in Grand Forks, North Dakota, attempts to distribute to a wider market by becoming one of the first to use new videotex technology.

When you've finished meeting these people and learning about their businesses, you'll see that in many cases they can't even begin to worry about selling before they know how they're going to get their product to market in the first place.

Chapter Twenty

Catalog Sales: Making Book

For a smaller to midsize company with a burgeoning list of new products or services, sometimes catalogs prove to be an inexpensive and effective means to hit the market.

CATALOG CONCENTRATION

For PRO-ED, an Austin, Texas-based publisher of education and testing materials geared towards the special education market, catalogs have been the key to growth from a company doing $30,000 in gross sales when it began in 1977 to between $3 and $4 million in 1984.

Steve Mathews, vice president of PRO-ED, says, "Our marketing is not overly sophisticated, but it's worked very, very well. Our main vehicle is a catalog of all products. We mail it twice a year, dropping around 500,000 or 600,000 catalogs to potential buyers."

Mathews and Donald Hammill, president and founder of PRO-ED, look at how much it costs to produce and mail the catalog. Then they check to see if sales have gone up or down. The percentage of money against total revenues PRO-ED uses every year on advertising is now around 5 percent, all concentrated on the catalog.

PRO-ED's catalog now features more than 600 titles, ranging from tests such as "TONI—The Test of Nonverbal Intelligence" to books such as *Does Your Child Have Epilepsy?*

"We avoid conventional publishing tactics," Hammill boasts. When asked about market research, he explains, "Mr. Mathews and I ask our buddies and friends, and that's what we go with. Education of the handicapped is our focus. It helps to be pretty much enmeshed in my field. We don't really do any market research."

Hammill and Mathews certainly are enmeshed in the field. Mathews was for about 15 years an editor of educational books at Allyn & Bacon, Inc., so he's got a good sense of the educational book market. Hammill was more directly involved in the field as a professor of special education. He had retired to Austin from Philadelphia, but not with the idea of growing what he now hopes will be a $10 million dollar company by 1987. Like a lot of entrepreneurial spirits, Hammill was faced with a potential gold mine of an idea, and, rather than remain in retirement, he seized the opportunity.

The company had its roots in a meeting in 1977 between a former student and Hammill. The student approached him with the idea for a product. "We needed a distribution arm," says Hammill. "So we formed a partnership to sell the product we had developed. I had other friends who had products, so we formed more partnerships. We started the company with no money at all."

To handle start-up production costs, PRO-ED was run like a co-op: authors paid production costs and PRO-ED paid all other costs, including marketing, accounting, and warehousing. Sales for the first year were $34,000. "We're very careful of the products we take. Each one had to sell well or we would've sunk," Mathews says.

Because the authors took an added risk, PRO-ED hiked the royalty percentage. "If we're doing a co-op arrangement, we'll typically give the author 60 percent of the sales, and we'll take 40 percent," says Mathews. Now the company does very little co-op publishing and that's hiked PRO—ED's margins. "The company will now grow like topsy," enthuses Hammill, "because the 300 other titles we acquired are on typical 'slave contracts,' where the authors only get 5-to-15 percent."

Folding Acquisitions into a Master Catalog

PRO-ED has generated enough cash to acquire other companies, including H&H Enterprises in Lawrence, Kansas, Bobbs-Merrill's test division in Indianapolis, University Park Press in Baltimore, Maryland, and three or four journals. When the companies are acquired PRO-ED buys the products, not the staffs.

"We buy a company's product line which may be under-marketed and over produced," Hammill explains. "The selling company has already eaten the production costs. Once a product is developed, we don't need the staff. It costs us virtually nothing to add products to our catalog."

"We get from 20-to-50 letters-a-day requesting our catalog," Mathews says. The market consists of public schools, diagnostic clinics, people in private practice, colleges, and other educational groups.

Growth Outpaces Catalog Costs

PRO-ED's catalog is fairly massive, with 600 titles of tests, books, and journals intertwined. It's like reading a Sears Roebuck catalog geared towards special education publishing. But there's a reason behind lumping it all together.

"We've seen no pattern in the buying," says Mathews. "They mix and match so much that we want to let them have a choice. The average order is usually around $100-to-$125, which consists of three or four line items. We keep upping the number of catalogs we send out. The growth keeps outpacing the cost of doing the catalogs. We know there's going to be a point of diminishing returns, but as long as the percentage of costs against gross sales continues to get lower, we'll keep increasing the number of catalogs we mail out."

ICING ON THE CAKE

Not every company using catalogs as a marketing tool places all its marketing eggs in one catalog. Often, catalogs are used as a supplement to other means of selling, whether it be direct mail on individual products, storefront retail sales, or various other means of getting the marketing message to the street.

Boomerang, the vintage clothing shop in Montclair, New Jersey, caters to a teenage/college market. To supplement retail sales at its store on Bloomfield Avenue, owner Sue Fitzpatrick put together an inexpensive catalog featuring items from the store that would be easy to fulfill.

"We started doing mail order in early 1985," Fitzpatrick says. "When I had a herniated disk and was in bed last year, I started the mail order."

Capturing Names for Catalog Mail

To capture names to send her catalog to, Fitzpatrick runs an ad in the classified section of *Rolling Stone* magazine. The ad, which differs from issue-to-issue, and usually runs around six lines, costs around $200 for each placement. From the first ad she ran, Fitzpatrick culled around 400 names.

The ads are geared toward the market, capitalizing on current market trends and whatever happens to be hot. A recent ad read:

> "FINGERLESS LACE GLOVES. Black or white. Wrist $8/Elbows $10; Black lace pantyhose S, M, L $9. $1.50 postage. Send check/money order: Boomerang,

416 Bloomfield Avenue, Montclair, NJ 07042. Crazy Catalog $1."

The "Crazy Catalog" is 15-pages, inexpensively produced (xerox, one-sided, stapled together with pictures of tee-shirts, watches, lace gloves, and other Boomerang products), and obviously gives Fitzpatrick a much wider potential market than does her lone store on Bloomfield Avenue.

"One girl in Crete, Illinois, is a regular customer," Fitzpatrick explains, a bit amazed at how far-reaching her catalogs have been. "She got our ad in *Rolling Stone* and wrote me letters. She's 18. I still send her samples of things. Her family owns a video store out there. Usually her orders are around $75."

Not a Major Investment

"Everything I have in the catalog, I have in the store, so it wasn't a major investment," Fitzpatrick explains. The one change she had to make was learning to keep closer control of the inventory on items like tee-shirts, which sell particularly well in the catalog.

PEDDLING THE GOODS

Half of the customers that Bike Virginia takes on its bicycle tours come from catalog inquiries.

"You have to know how to spend your marketing dollars wisely," says Allen Turnbull, president of Bike Virginia. "As soon as you start putting ads in *Bicycling* magazine, you'll get requests for advertising from other magazines. You have to watch the return you get for every advertising dollar you spend."

Turnbull, who is 37, grew up in Hampton, Virginia, not far from Williamsburg. When he was in graduate school at William & Mary in the early 70s, he remembers he "had one of those new fangled 10-speeds." It wasn't until he went for his Ph.D. in Ottawa that he became a real bicycle enthusiast. "There are over 100 miles of bike paths up there," he remembers. "That really got me interested."

When he returned to Williamsburg, Turnbull found very few places in town to cycle. With three men friends and one woman friend, he put together Bike Virginia.

Bike Virginia, based in Williamsburg, has indeed watched its marketing dollars judiciously, because, at first, there weren't all that many dollars to spread around. In 1981, Turnbull and four of his friends put a total of $15,000 into Bike Virginia. Each year, they put all of their profits back into the bicycle touring company. With the exception of Turnbull, who recently left his job as a management consultant with James City County and now works as a free-lance consultant, they've all kept their full-time jobs in other fields. Sales in 1984 were around $50,000-a-year for trips ranging in price from $145-to-$365. That's for a base of roughly 300 customers, up more than 70 percent over the previous year. "In time, if the company doubles each year," says Turnbull, "in six or seven years we're talking $1 million in gross sales."

The key to doing well in this business, he says, is getting information into the bicycle shops. Most touring companies either have a little flier or postcards that you can send back to the company to receive a catalog. Bike Virginia sent out 75,000 fliers in 1984.

"There are probably about 2,000 bike shops' names available on computerized lists," Turnbull estimates. "Maybe 1,000 of those carry fliers in their shops. Bike stores have racks with brochures from all over the country. I think they see it as good marketing for themselves to carry the fliers. There are probably 5,000 premium bike shops you want to offer in."

Tracking the Source of Catalog Requests

Bike Virginia codes all of the fliers it sends out to bicycle shops, so it knows where the fliers are coming from, who's putting them out, and when to replenish a bicycle shop's supply. Its mailing list of individuals has grown to 5,000, drawn chiefly from the fliers that were sent in requesting the full catalog.

"Half of our customers come from the inquiries," says Turnbull. "The other half comes from ads we place in *Bicycling* magazine, *Outside* magazine, and various trade magazines, plus word-of-mouth." The ads cost around $5,000 a year.

The company will print 10,000 catalogs and 75,000 fliers-a-year. The catalogs cost about $6,000; the fliers, $2,000.

There's a lot of competition among bicycle touring companies, but it doesn't worry Turnbull. "I think there's an expanding market, with each company helping each other along the way. It's not going to be a matter of the top sodas fighting it out for a market share."

MARKETING MESSAGES

In an age of sexy ads, catalogs still count. Catalogs are an inexpensive, effective message to your market. Combined with direct mail, responses can be tracked and fine-tuned. You know who's ordering what, and you can alter the next catalog to fit market demand.

More catalogs can mean increased business. As long as the production costs remain in-line with gross sales, the bold entrepreneur should consider increasing the number of catalogs mailed each year. Some, like PRO-ED, find that the percentage of catalog costs against gross sales grows smaller each year.

Catalogs can supplement other types of sales. Retail shops use them to pitch products to an untapped market. The key is wise use of marketing dollars. If catalog marketing isn't really cost-effective, consider other methods.

Chapter Twenty–One

Distributing it to Market: Nice and Easy Does It

For any entrepreneur trying to sell a product, smooth and efficient distribution to the market is crucial. It's obvious that if the product doesn't get to market the customer can't buy it, and the producer can't sell it.

While distribution methods differ, the underlying purpose transcends industry lines. Occasionally, shortages of a product seem to increase the demand for it, like the "Cabbage Patch Doll" craze or the 'Trivial Pursuit" mania. But for the small to midsize businessperson it makes little sense to try to withhold a product to create demand. Get the products out there and let the market buy.

Good distribution methods aren't always an assurance, however, that products will be distributed efficiently. Sometimes a company's popular products will overshadow the lesser known lines when they're being brought to market. Near East Foods,

Inc.'s president, Jack Kalajian, says that one of the biggest distribution problems he has is that Near East's rice pilaf is selling so well. "We'll have eight-to-ten facings of rice pilaf on a grocery shelf, and only one facing of our Spanish rice," he explains.

Direct Distribution or Brokers?

To keep its lesser known products from being shuffled into obscurity on the grocery shelf, Near East uses two methods of distribution: Distributing directly to a food wholesaler or the supermarkets, or, more preferably, using a food broker. Sometimes, when it has to, Near East will use a specialty food distributor.

"In the marketplace, we used to be unsure of proper shelf space and accurate pricing," says Walter Moquin, Near East's vice president of sales and marketing. "We now use regional food brokers. We and other manufacturers give brokers a legal monopoly to sell our product in a given region. We pay him a commission. He also represents Pillsbury, Progresso, Best Food, and Campbell's specialty items.

"The broker makes sure that our product is there to sell. He's not just important to us, but also to the supermarket. The broker ends up acting as an extension of our marketing and sales department."

There are about 75 regions that food brokers represent throughout the United States. Moquin figures that by the end of 1987, Near East will be represented in each region. In those areas where the company is not now represented by a broker it will sell directly to wholesalers or retailers.

Near East tries not to get placed in the specialty item sections of supermarkets. But since its products are not all that familiar yet, sometimes it's been the only way to get into the stores. With names like couscous, wheat pilaf, felafel, sesame tahini, and taboule among its products it's sometimes difficult to get in the dry grains section of a store where Near East prefers to be.

"The product has evolved to the point of warranting direct sales," Moquin insists. "We want it in the dry grain sections of grocery stores, because our products are basically carbohydrate substitutes."

Producing Product and Getting it to the Buyer

Not all distribution methods are mired in the same complexity that Near East Foods faces. Some companies don't have the worries of brokers or wholesalers, but simply need to get the product produced and out to the buyer. Marblehead Kite Company of Marblehead, Massachusetts, is one such example.

Marblehead Kites is headquartered three flights up in a large, old yellow building on Pleasant Street. Marblehead is one of those rustic seaport towns that brings in hundreds of tourists during the summer.

Betty Breuhaus is the owner and founder of the company, which reports about $100,000 in annual sales. Marblehead Kites are carried all over the country in kite stores, department stores, high quality gift shops, and through limited mail order catalogs. Its strongest presence, however, is in New England, which accounts for 50 percent of sales, and Texas, which accounts for 25 percent of sales.

Like many entrepreneurs, Breauhaus sort of "happened" into her business through a stroke of coincidence. "When I was vacationing in California in the early 1970s, I knew I wanted to come back, but I had dislocated my shoulder while I was skiing so I couldn't drive back. I walked into a kite store and picked up a Japanese kite. Some guy came up to me and said, 'I know where you can get that for half the price.' He wrote down an address and gave me a piece of paper. It was the address of people making cloth kites in San Francisco.

"When I got to the address, which turned out to be Whitebird Kites, the man said, 'We don't sell kites, but we'll show them to you.' I convinced them to sell me a windrider and asked them if they'd make me an apprentice for two weeks if I gave them the labor for free."

Breuhaus learned the kite business, came home to Marblehead, and started the Marblehead Kite Company.

Whitebird Kites has since moved to Hawaii. "They do make the prettiest kites," Breuhaus sighs.

"I went on a real binge in the late 1970s," says Breuhaus. "I was in about six mail order catalogs, three of which went out of business. We limit it to places like Land's End and Horchow's catalogs now. You're not going to get burned there."

Breuhaus uses brokers, sells to kite specialty shops herself, and produces a catalog which she sends to wholesale buyers. The catalog gets mailed out every January.

"The catalogs are done by an outfit in New York," says Breuhaus. "They do the photography, typesetting, color separations, and printing for about $1,600 for 2,000 catalogs."

Limiting Selection to Meet Demands

One of the main distribution problems Breuhaus faced came as a result of offering a wide selection of kites. Come peak season for kite buying—June through August—Marblehead Kites would sometimes have a difficult time knowing what to keep in stock to keep up with demand. To handle the quagmire of paper that would often fly in the door, Breuhaus began limiting the selection of kites offered in the catalog.

"When the kite stores order in June through August, they need the stuff immediately," she says. "Sometimes it's a problem, so I decided to simplify to help know what to keep in stock by beginning to offer a limited selection, about two-thirds as many as before. That way it'll be easier to fill orders.

"I've realized sitting up here that I can't dictate what I want to make," she adds. "I have to listen to kite sellers, get out there and see what they want." To make sure the sellers' desires don't foul the distribution works too much by wanting the world, Breuhaus limits selection. Give them what they want—but not so much that they won't be able to have it.

"Our kites are not like normal kites," muses Breuhaus. "They're kind of like 'upper-middle class' kites," she says, referring to the fact that her kites are in the $10-to-$20 dollar range and not just used for flying, but also for decorative purposes.

To keep up with the production demand and to keep overhead low, Breuhaus only has one full-time production person working with her. The bulk of production is completed from the cottage industry of stitchers Breuhaus has set up. These stitchers work out of their homes, cutting patterns and stitching kites together. They are paid by the piece and range in number from six to twenty at any given time, depending upon the search and the demand.

The Charm of the Product

"Some of the charm of the Marblehead kite is that it's not too slick," says Breuhaus. "We're the only company doing cotton kites." She notes that recently she has moved to making kites of mylar material which not only carry over the decorative qualities, but also add "flyability." The mylar kite was offered to meet the market demand.

"Kites are such a mystery to people that when they walk into a retail store, the salesperson really has a hold on the customer," says Breuhaus, joking that a typical sales pitch might be, "This is a Marblehead kite. There's a little old lady in Marblehead who makes these." Breuhaus is in her mid-thirties.

Marblehead Kite, which Breuhaus started in 1974, also designs and manufactures windsocks. Breuhaus believes that the windsocks present some good opportunity for growth in sales. "I really think the windsock market is open," she says, noting that she plans to begin marketing promotional windsocks, particularly to the marine market.

While the designs on the kites and windsocks are changed every year to "add variety and keep interest," Breuhaus notes that the idea on kites and windsocks is to make the color and shape work so the design doesn't have to be too intricate. The more intricate, the more time it takes to produce, resulting in slow production rates, which Breuhaus has learned to avoid if she wants to distribute efficiently during those peak summer months.

In the spring and summer months, Marblehead Kite opens a retail shop selling mostly seconds and discontinued items from space on the second floor of its Pleasant Street building. The operation has met with good success and profit, according to Breuhaus.

"Our market niche is cotton kites, windsocks, and mylar kites," Breuhaus explains. "Everything's made here. The materials are mostly from Boston. In fact, the original fellow I bought material from was named Ben Franklin. He's retired now."

While competition in the kite market is increasing, particularly with some big players capturing large shares of the market on both coasts—"Go Fly a Kite" out of New York City and "Spectra Star" out of Encino, California—Breuhaus is optimistic that Marblehead Kite, with its charm and quality, will continue to carve out a niche for itself in the marketplace.

"Kites are so basic and so much fun," says Breuhaus. "They're not going to go away." With effective distribution methods, Breuhaus would like to make sure of that.

MARKETING MESSAGES

Be there when the market says so. If you're not there when the market wants your product you're out of luck—or out of business.

Use brokers as an extension of your marketing department. In the case of small businesses, brokers *are* the marketing department. Make sure they reflect what you want reflected in the marketplace. Give them the right information and tools to work with.

Be sure you can deliver what you say you will. You're biting off more than you can chew if distribution can't keep up with your offerings.

Sometimes less is more. If the market is just as great if you produce fewer products or services, consider limiting what you have to sell. If you try to offer too much you may lose your market share.

Chapter Twenty-Two

Using Videotex: Screening the Market

Silverman's Inc., had been selling shirts and suits in Grand Forks, North Dakota, about the same way for more than 70 years. It is, says vice president Stephen Silverman, the largest men's clothing store in North Dakota. One location, one market, with sales of, according to Silverman, "under $3 million, but substantially more than $2 million."

Now all that has changed.

In the fall of 1983, Silverman tapped into Viewtron, a videotex shop-at-home system that Viewdata Corp. of America, a wholly-owned subsidiary of Knight-Ridder Newspapers Inc., operates in southeast Florida.

"I came across an article in the paper about Knight-Ridder conducting an experiment in videotex," recalls Silverman. "The local paper in Grand Forks is owned by Knight-Ridder, and Mike Maidenberg, the publisher, got me in touch with them. We signed a contract with Viewtron in July 1983, and went live in December 1983."

Silverman set up a separate corporation, Essential Clothiers Corp., which has the same clothing lines as the original store, but offers them electronically to an entirely new group of customers. As Silverman, who also is president of Essential Clothiers, puts it, he has, in effect, created a new store without having to worry about staff, inventory, sales space, or any of the other problems that the Silverman family has wrestled with for more than seven decades. Essential Clothiers is simply another marketing outlet for the same inventory that Silverman's stocks.

New Opportunities for Smaller Businesses

The new venture is not without its problems. But the long-awaited advent of videotex and other electronic marketing systems can offer startling new opportunities to small companies. In the case of Silverman's, the new marketing option promises to transform the entire company. While there are only 45,000 people in Grand Forks and 650,000 in all of North Dakota, there are some 1.6 million in metropolitan Miami alone. "The potential exists for Essential Clothiers to become bigger than our retail operation. We could become a major national company without ever opening another store," says Silverman. "We can be in business 24-hours-a-day, seven-days-a-week, and we don't need someone to be available to take orders or wait on customers."

Viewtron subscribers can call up a display of Essential Clothiers' wares on home television by using special keyboards and telephone line connections. The orders are punched in directly by consumers and nearly all are entered during the night or at other times when customers are not usually out shopping.

"We check the order index at least once a day," Silverman says, "generally early in the morning." The customer is then sent a confirmation electronically to verify that the order has been received. The confirmation is personalized, allowing Essential Clothiers to achieve a "high tech/high touch" relationship. "We promise shipping within 24 hours from the time the confirmation was sent, 48 hours if alterations are needed."

Still a Test Operation

So far, sales have been slow, but Silverman considers Essential Clothiers to be a test operation. He thinks it will take roughly three-to-five years to make money on the videotex operation because it requires further research to refine and perfect it.

"We're spending more time analyzing than doing the business," Silverman explains. "Say we retail the merchandise for $35 and theoretically it costs us $17.50. Well, we're probably spending another $20-to-$25 worth of time, phone money, and everything else to find out why the customer bought the product and who they are. We've invested just a shade over $30,000 at this point since we started. It's going to take around 25,000 subscribers on this system before we break even. There are now probably around 4,000 total subscribers."

Approaching Videotex as a Major Player

Silverman explains that one of the reasons he was so attracted to videotex is that the "future for small business is bleak. The market share is shrinking as big businesses move in and exploit the market to the fullest. The ability to have a small business and even more than a modest income is going to be difficult. We have to approach what we do as a major player in the primary and secondary markets. We consider ourselves a major player with videotex. If we didn't, Sears, Penneys, and IBM would sweep the medium. Before you know it, every home will have one of these terminals dialing directly into major marketers and bypassing the little guys. I don't want to be one of those little guys. I want to be one of those people who the mass market consumer is accessing."

Originally, Essential Clothiers offered Viewtron customers a broad range of clothing with not much depth in brands and styles so that Silverman could get a feel for what the customers would want. In the future, the new company plans to tailor its offerings to the new market.

"We'll start to narrow down the range and go into greater depth," Silverman says. "If dress shirts seem to be the hot thing, we'll try to have the most complete offering [customers] can find anywhere."

"Our very early going experience was very depressing," he confides. "We were going weeks without activity. That was a real downer. But it made us knuckle-down and start disciplining ourselves to do things right."

Despite the long wait for an initial payoff, Silverman is now enthusiastic about videotex as a marketing vehicle. It is, he says, "a perfect way for a small business to grow, as long as they understand the system."

When Times Mirror launched its consumer videotex system called "Gateway" in Orange County, California, in November 1984, Essential Clothiers entered the southern California market.

"Gateway still has a small subscriber base, but it's growing at a faster rate off the block than Viewtron did. Although we're nowhere near satisfied, overall growth is optimistic. In 1984 we did 10-times the business we did in 1983. This year we've already done half of what we did last year. We're growing at a faster rate, but our numbers are still in the red. In February of 1985, our cash flow for the first time exceeded expenses," Silverman explains.

Since Viewtron only got up and going at the end of 1983, the fact that Essential Clothiers did 10-times the business in 1984 than it did during the previous year is not terribly surprising. The positive cash flow in the early months of 1985, however, may indeed be an indication that things are looking up for Essential Clothiers' videotex operation.

How Videotex Works

The importance of videotex has been predicted for years, but it is only recently that the systems have begun to move out of the pilot phase. Videotex is an interactive system in which a subscriber can shop at home using a specially designed terminal and a television screen. Customers can use the system to seek out the goods and services they want, from appliances to gabardine slacks, then actually place orders over the same system.

A marketer, such as Essential Clothiers, buys space on the system by the "page," which corresponds to a full display screen. The pages might include graphic displays, lists of products, descriptions of the goods, or order information. Essential Clothiers, for example, has about 60 pages on the Viewtron system. The first page carries a picture of a double-breasted sport coat, the Essential Clothiers logo, and an index of all the clothes the company carries.

The pages also include a questionnaire called "Nobody Just Like You," which covers clothing sizes, such tailoring preferences as cuffs on trousers, and other information often needed in ordering. The customer completes the questionnaire and sends it to Essential Clothiers electronically. Then, to place an order, the customer simply checks a box on the order form notifying the company that the rest of the order information is already on file. It all happens simply, directly, and electronically.

Opportunity and Confusion

The new technology has brought a whole array of new marketing options to small businesses, offering vast opportunity as well as an element of confusion. Since most small businesses work with limited marketing budgets, any funds that go into newer—somewhat experimental—marketing vehicles might have to be taken away from more traditional advertising and promotion media.

"It's like going into the world's largest candy store. You've got your quarter and you want everything. But you're limited by what you can afford," says Benson P. Shapiro, professor of marketing at the Harvard University Graduate School of Business Administration. "Small businesses better think carefully about priorities and not move too quickly."

Yet the options are tantalizing. Viewtron, for example, is just one of a number of interactive electronic systems that allow for some sort of at-home shopping.

"The real potential advantage of videotex is that the message is communicated to the prospective customer on the same channel that can be used to place an order," claims Roger Strang, a visiting associate professor of marketing at New York University.

Upscale Market

Knight-Ridder's Viewdata Corp. of America was the first to offer full service with its Viewtron system. It was introduced in October 1983, after a lengthy test, to a potential 1.3 million households in southeastern Florida. Viewtron's goal in the first year of operation was to establish at least 5,000 subscribers in the Miami area, a mark which apparently fell short. The bulk of the market is assumed to be families with male heads of household from the ages of 25-to-49 with yearly incomes of $35,000 or more each—an upscale market profile sought by virtually all the players that have entered the videotex field.

That is why Miami auto dealer Mike Seidle is using videotex. Seidle, a vice president of Bill Seidle's Datsun/Bill Seidle's Miami Mitsubishi, has been using Viewtron for several months. So far, sales have been somewhat limited, in large part because the subscriber base is still small, Seidle says. But he thinks it "can work for small businesses because the markets are targeted. You're not paying for national exposure."

A Great Equalizer

Penny Welsch, manager of marketing communications for Times-Mirror Videotex Services' Gateway system, predicts that videotex will be a "great equalizer," putting smaller companies on a much more equal footing with their larger competitors.

"A big retailer is not going to have a lot more prominence than a local merchant," Welsch explains. "We're going to offer local shopping mall merchants in Orange County a very reasonably priced package allowing a certain number of pages which include information about their stores. We also set them up with videotex terminals with which they can create or alter their own ads at their own discretion."

Steve Silverman concurs. "There's no reason we can't grow as much as multimillion dollar retailers like Sears. Look at our market. Look at how many people they can reach. In the videotex system, we're on the same level with the big guys. The opportunity is there for a small business like ours to grow."

Silverman adds that Times-Mirror's Gateway system has another experimental system called HBI (Home Banking Interchange), on which Essential Clothiers gets carried. The HBI is an experiment being run in conjunction with banks in 16 different cities, broadening Essential Clothiers' market potential.

Instantaneous Medium

"It's such an instantaneous medium as opposed to direct mail," Robin Silverman says. Robin is Steve's wife and advertising director for Silverman's. She adds that Gateway has also been more advertiser-oriented than its competitor, Viewtron, which to-date has been very consumer-oriented. Robin says Gateway has advertising for sale on almost every page. The front of the menu costs about $400 a week. Others go from $100 to $200 a week. "They'll sell anything. You want something, they'll put a price on it," she says.

Some Technological Problems

But videotex is not without its troubles. Currently, the systems operate over telephone lines and that doesn't allow for the glamourous videos possible on service's like The Cableshop, a 24-hour-a-day, all-commercial, interactive cable channel now operating in limited test markets nationwide, or Qube, an interactive cable system that has been hitting more than 250,000 subscribers in six test markets (Chicago, St. Louis, Houston, Dallas, Cincinnati, and Columbus, Ohio) for more than seven years. But the cable systems haven't rolled out into full operation yet.

"Two-way cable just isn't ready," insists James Holly, president of Times-Mirror Videotex Services. "We tested two-way cable in 1982, and it worked. But to do it on a large scale, a lot of work has to be done. The equipment, the software, the networking, the reliability is just not there in most of these cable systems. It will be over time, but it'll be at least two-to-five years."

These telephone line systems, however, currently rely on a dedicated terminal developed by American Telephone & Telegraph Co. called Sceptre. Viewtron subscribers have had to purchase the control keyboard for $600, but the company just began offering the option of renting a terminal for $39.95-a-month. Gateway included the rental of the Sceptre as part of a $30 monthly fee for the first 2,000 subscribers in Orange County.

Neither Viewtron nor Gateway has developed the software to adapt home computers into receivers of the videotex information. According to John Borden, senior analyst with the Boston-based consulting and market research firm Yankee Group, "it was a major error, failing to ride piggyback on the excitement of having a computer in the home."

Yankee Group predicts that by the end of 1984, around 13.1 million homes in America will have purchased computers; 12 percent of these will have purchased the modems necessary to receive the videotex services over telephone lines. By 1988, Yankee Group believes the numbers will at least double.

The question of using the home computer to receive the videotex services may have been answered emphatically in February 1984, when CBS, IBM, and Sears, Roebuck announced a joint venture to begin development of a commercial videotex service to households with home or personal computers.

It will be several years before the CBS-IBM-Sears system, called "Trintron," is up and running. But Borden believes that "we're on the verge of something new, because the medium has attracted the sophisticated players now. Over the past several years, videotex has sputtered and dragged on—a whole lot of noise but not a whole lot of money has been made."

Getting a Leg Up on Competition

The very novelty of the videotex system, however, might be a plus for some marketers. Professor Shapiro of Harvard sees two distinct advantages to being on the forefront. The first is that "sometimes the first people in just buy it cheaper because these people are all pretty hungry. The second is that sometimes you can really get a leg up on your competition and develop a whole new way of marketing."

Steve Silverman believes he is getting out in front of the competition. "In the latest research," he boasts, "it showed that in the number of sessions people used Viewtron per-month, we were in the top five. In our category, fashion products, we're number two.

"I don't regret my decision to use videotex at all."

MARKETING MESSAGES

Videotex, the "Great Equalizer." "This new system can work for the small company trying to go up against behemoth retail competition. You don't have to be huge to be a major player in this market, and it's a great growth vehicle.

Videotex, the "Expander." "No one knows just how big the market expansion potential will be. A store in North Dakota, a state with only a 650,000 population, can plug into 1.6 million buyers in the Miami market alone.

Don't let the "bugs" chase you away. Like all new technology, videotex can't guarantee it will succeed. But the entrepreneur willing to take a risk may be getting in on the ground floor of an exciting new marketing outlet—a part of the future.

Maxim Six

The Selling Code

Sell Hard. Sell Often.

Throughout the journey, I've stressed that marketing consists of more than selling. I've not meant, however, to belittle the role that selling plays in the whole process. In the chapters that follow, you'll see the importance of selling all too clearly.

The thrust of the book so far has been on the marketing techniques used by small to midsize businesses. The result of successful marketing, of course, translates into the sale of products and services, the bottom line of all business. If you examine the components of marketing you will see two distinct accomplishments: 1. bringing a product to market; 2. making the market aware of its need for that product.

The chapters that follow give a taste of what goes into the selling process. You'll see how various businesses deal with issues ranging from pricing to selling techniques to managing sales staffs. You'll sit with me through one of the many sales pitches I faced, and learn some of the philosophy behind the pitch. And, in Boonton, New Jersey, you'll sense the magic of the old-time sell.

All of the hard work—the commitment to giving the market what it wants, not compromising on quality, experimenting with new technology, making sure the products are available for the customer to buy—comes to naught if the product doesn't sell. Ultimately, it takes purchases to bring in the money that keeps a business running.

In this last section, you'll meet many of the businesspeople who you might remember meeting in earlier chapters. What follows is a "slice of sales life" for many of them. It may spell a business' ultimate success, but selling cannot work alone. There's got to be some steak behind the sizzle if you want the customers to come back for more.

Chapter Twenty-Three

The Price is Right

You've got the product or service, added a few bells and whistles, targeted the market, achieved the correct image in the marketplace, and figured out a way to get the product to market. What'll you charge for it? Some number pulled out of the air because you feel it's just as appropriate as any other? Or some number based on *something?*

James Tobak, self-styled eccentric and premier magazine consultant, charges an hourly consulting fee of $423. He told Judith Adler Hennessee in a recent *Manhattan, Inc.* article: "I'm trying to be the highest in the world. I am in the marketing business. If you sell retail, you never end up with an even number."

Arbitrary pricing doesn't always work, but sometimes it does. Merrill Diamond, who runs the Brookline, Massachusetts, real estate development company called Parencorp says that when he and his fellow architect and partner, Gordon Hurwitz, started their real estate development projects, "We made as many mistakes in the first building as we could on a project. Next to doctors, architects are the worst businessmen on earth.

"We used to price by saying, 'This is a nice unit, what do you think someone would pay for it?' Because we did stuff like architects, we didn't pay attention to costs. As interest rates went up to 20 percent, our expensive units sold well because our market could afford it. [They didn't need to rely on exorbitant mortgage rates available at the time.] Now we make a conscious decision to go after a wealth market," Diamond says. No doubt his arbitrary pricing strategy paid off in the long run.

But arbitrariness doesn't always spell success. With Parencorp and other savvy entrepreneurs, it can often be pulled off through good timing, last minute maneuvers, and a slick presentation. But for other companies who rely on a regular body of products for income, its typically best to rely on a regular pricing method.

The Impact of Pricing on Sales

Some, like Dennis Sylvester, follow a "basic rule-of-thumb" as their regular pricing method. Sylvester, president of American Metal Fabricators, the sheet metal fabrication division of Hudson Industries, Hudson, New Hampshire, bases his pricing on the following logic: "If I know I can do it for a dollar and they'll pay two dollars, I'll charge them two dollars. Then in bad times, I can go back and offer it at a buck-and-a-half." In 1984, the profit structure of American Metal tripled over the previous year. Sylvester's theory of pricing no doubt helped.

A company's pricing structure can have a significant impact on its sales. First, it can help a company gain firmer control of what it costs to make a product or deliver a service. Pricing structure also tells how much a customer is going to have to pay to make it worth continuing production. Second, it gives an idea of just how valuable an entrepreneur's wares are to the outside world.

When Bob Roen, executive editor and vice president of Bankers Publishing, joined the company back in 1982, one of the first things he did with Tim Warren, the company's president and part owner, was to rethink the pricing structure on the books the company publishes and markets to banking professionals. Examining the pricing structure, "is probably the most significant thing that's accounted for our sales increase," says Roen, in his South Street office. "We significantly increased our product prices, sometimes as much as 100 percent.

"Generally in the past when the book was published an adequate price was set, and it was not changed until a reprint was done. In some cases Bankers had printed enough to last three or four years. In my opinion, that's wrong, because other costs will have increased. So in 1982, we had a major increase in prices. We also decided that once a year we'd examine books for possible price increases."

Decisions Based on Entrepreneurship

Other businesses face similar problems with costs increasing while prices remain fairly stagnant. Al Felly of Felly's Flowers in Madison, Wisconsin, says, "Our business is blessed with a times mark-up situation. When I started in business, the keystone was a three-to-one markup on flowers and two-to-one on non-perishables." The pricing hasn't kept up, however.

Felly sees a solution. "The basic thought is entrepreneurship," says Felly. "Is it such a big thing to look at the bottom of a financial statement and say, 'This is what to charge if we're going to make a profit?' Make decisions based on entrepreneurship."

"You want to run a business?" Felly asks. "Then run a business."

When Bankers Publishing first published the seventh edition of its anchor book, the *Encyclopedia of Banking and Finance*, in 1973, it was priced at $49.50. Eight years later, it was still selling for $49.50. "In 1982, we raised the price of the eighth edition to $89 and plan to increase it to $94 in 1985," says Bob Roen.

Look at Product Profit and Loss

"We now do a profit and loss on each book," Roen says, explaining how Bankers ultimately arrives at whether or not to publish a book, let alone what to charge for it. "We start out with what we think the perceived value is for each book. We work in all of the other variables [such as product development, royalties, order processing, composition, marketing]. If it doesn't work, we're faced with choices. We can change the costs or we can charge more."

Costs obviously play a major role in the pricing procedure. When Roen lists "changing the costs" as one of his choices, he obviously doesn't mean arbitrarily changing the costs on a sheet of paper; he means looking to see if he can find someone to supply particular services or materials at a cheaper price.

Sue Fitzpatrick, owner of Boomerang's, the vintage clothing store in Montclair, New Jersey, follows the same policy on a much smaller scale. When rubber bracelets got real "in" with her teenage customers, she decided that the fashion accessories distributors were charging her too much for the product.

"I like to go straight to the person who makes them, rather than an expensive new-wave distributor," says Fitzpatrick. "I go straight to the O-ring manufacturer — they're gaskets from cars — and get them for 6 cents each instead of 17 cents. I sell them for 50 cents. I've sold thousands."

Perceived Value

But prudence must be exercised when entertaining lower cost substitutes. Sure you'd like to get it cheaper, but you don't want to buy junk and lose the perceived value of your product to the consumer. Hal Gershman, who owns Happy Harry's Bottle Shop in Grand Forks, North Dakota, says he'll negotiate for closeouts on liquors, "but we'll only do quality closeouts. We won't buy garbage just to have a cheap price."

Roen admits that back in 1982, when Bankers was just building up its list of titles, the company did a few books just to generate enough cash flow to sink into future products. It was worth it to take a risk on the profitability of some books at the outset, because these books would still bring in enough to develop blockbuster titles that would keep the company in gravy in later years.

Profit Analysis

While Merrill Diamond of Parencorp now gets computer updates with cost analyses of his various real estate development projects, he's also quite adept these days at figuring out just how much he'll spend and make on a building.

"Take the example of a double unit row house in the Back Bay [of Boston]. The acquisition cost would be around $400,000. There'll be a total project cost of around $2.2 million —20,000 square feet at a cost of $110-a-square-foot. Of that, say the typical unit has 1,750 saleable square feet and there are ten units. That's 17,500 square feet. Say it's selling in the range of $200-a-square-foot. That'll be a total sell-out of $3.5 million. A total profit of $1.3 million."

Not everyone can rattle off numbers like Diamond. And even he relies on sophisticated software programs to prove his gut instinct correct.

Bob Roen and others at Bankers Publishing usually have a good idea what their products will sell for, but they will always do a price analysis four times during the course of a book's development — prior to contract signing, once the manuscript is received, after the book is set in type, and within six weeks after the book has been published. Although there's often a year-and-a-half between signing and actual publication, says Roen, "If we've done it correctly, the price shouldn't vary too much at the four times."

Roen pulls out the pricing sheet for a recent book called *Work Measurement in Banking*. In November 1982, the company priced it at $37 when it signed the contract. In November 1983, Bankers projected that the price would be between $39 and $42. In December 1983, when the book was about to go to the printer, the price remained between $39 and $42. When it was finally published in July 1984, it had a list price of $39, only two dollars over the price they figured on two years earlier.

Roen says the marketing department at Bankers plays an important role in pricing its books. "I try to get our marketing manager to buy into the project long before it's even committed, so we don't walk into the same situation other publishing companies find themselves in where the sales manager says, 'I can't sell this book.' "It's a little Machiavellian, but we do get the marketing department sold on the project before the book is developed."

Marketing Messages

Price for profit. Determine costs, judge value, and analyze exactly what you have to charge to make it pay.

Stagnant prices leave you flat. At regular intervals evaluate your pricing. Does it still reflect its real value to market? If not, change the price.

Get your salespeople to buy into the product up-front. Whoever will be selling for you should be involved in pricing, if at all possible. By having them buy into the product or service from the outset, you'll have their backing when it's time to go to market.

Chapter Twenty-Four

Sell Hard. Sell Often.

Natural Choice Industries, Inc. was founded by Gary R. Scaife and his wife, Marilyn, in 1981 as a sole proprietorship. They incorporated in 1982. The company is based in Westlake Village, California, one of the many towns, which, when you ask for directions, you get as a response, "You know, just outside of Los Angeles." Gary and Marilyn in less than five years grew their company to the point where, in 1984, Gary estimates gross sales were just over $5 million. Their chief products are fruit juices and snack food items.

They've managed to build up sales through a combination of marketing strategies. First they rely heavily on a distribution network built up from supplying generic brands to stores. Since the channels are there, they can also supply their own products. Second, they used the technique of licensing nationally known characters rather than try to start from scratch to advertise to a national market. Third, after they've pinpointed a market niche they believe they can do well in, they use their own sales brokers to sell their products to stores in that niche. And fourth, they used established manufacturers to make the products and also distribute them for a fee based on percentage of sales — in effect, bringing the manufacturer in as a minor partner in the deal.

They've sold hard; they've sold as often as they possibly could; and they've sold successfully. The selling instinct is implicit throughout my discussion with Gary Scaife.

"We're averaging just over 2 percent market share on lemonades and powder mixes," Gary Scaife tells me in his Westlake Village office, just outside Los Angeles. "We're now in eight states—Illinois, Michigan, New York, New Jersey, Pennsylvania, Iowa, Minnesota, and California. The powdered drink business is a very big business. It'll do about $800 million this year. We're not going to be placed everywhere. We're going to try to be in a niche in the big markets."

Powdered mixes are just one type of product carried by Natural Choice. Natural Choice Industries, Inc., is now the holding company for four separate divisions—Natural Choice Foods, which handles snack food items and a cat food the company plans to introduce; Popeye Fruit Juice Company, which handles production and distribution of the Popeye Fruit Juice line of products; Pink Panther Beverage Company, which handles the line of Pink Panther and Son drink mixes; and the International Beverage Corporation, which packages juices for other people.

"Number four is our bread-and-butter division," says Scaife. "It gets us into the distribution network. They know us from that. If we complete a project we're working on now, we'll acquire a major packager of drinks, and our fourth division will far and away be larger. Our main thrust, however, is our name brands divisions."

Licensing Well-Known Names to Build Recognition

Scaife reasons that it usually costs anywhere from $25 million to $50 million for a company to introduce a product nationally and to make it a name brand. "Pink Panther is already a name brand," says Scaife. "It's the number one show in America, a 'now' sort of character." So Scaife and his business associates figure it's worth it to them to pay for a license to use names like the Pink Panther (MGM-United Artists) or Popeye (King Features Syndicate), or Tom and Jerry (also MGM-UA) for their proposed cat food product.

"We'll throw out more than one and hope one sticks," says Scaife. He figures it will cost Natural Choice $2.5-to-$5 million to introduce a national product this way as opposed to $25-to-$30 million. "That's the only way a company of our size can succeed in the marketplace."

When I ask him if it gets expensive buying up licenses for various nationally recognized characters, Scaife responds, "As opposed to what we have to do to get a brand name? No. If we're wrong, no . . . not really. How many supermarket buyers do you think we'd get to talk to if we walked in with 'Gary's Mother's Juice?'"

While Scaife boasts that he "keeps the corporate staff pretty light," the company has made some heavyweight additions to staff since it began as a husband and wife team in 1981. Robert Held, president and chief operating officer of the holding company, was formerly in "high management" with RJ French and Anheiser-Busch. Also hired was a director of retail sales who had been director of retail sales for Joseph Schlitz Brewing Company's Midwest region. Scaife is director of advertising and chief executive officer, and Marilyn is director of advertising and promotions and president of one of the divisions.

"We intend to grow to $50 million in sales by 1990 with a combination of products that will become successful and the continuous introduction of new products. We're hoping to have twelve products on the market at any one time. Half will be year-to-year products, those that stick nationally," Scaife says.

Growth by continuous introduction of new products. He's selling hard. He's selling often.

Brokers or Manufacturers Get Product to Market

But Natural Choice has the same concerns as other companies. It has to get its product produced and get it on the shelves so consumers can buy it. "We try to market in two ways," says Scaife. "We either do it ourselves with our own brokers, or we sign an agreement with an established manufacturer of the product.

"We're basically a marketing company," he explains, "so we try to subcontract to have most of our products manufactured. The powedered drink mix manufacturer we use is the fourth largest manufacturer of powdered drink mixes in the United States. We're getting them to handle not only manufacturing, but also distribution. We handle all advertising and promotion. We pay the manufacturer a fee to manufacture the drink mix, plus a master broker fee. We get everything in between. Both fees to the manufacturer range between 9 percent and 11 percent of gross sales."

The "Chickens-In-One-Basket" Nightmare

Relying on an outside established manufacturer as a broker is not a bad idea, unless at some point down the road the manufacturer decides it is *too* established. Betty Breuhaus, owner of Marblehead Kite Company, the Marblehead, Massachusetts-based kite manufacturer, learned this the hard way. "Go Fly a Kite," a New York kite distributor which has been around for about 20 years, had been carrying her cotton kites for some time. "At one point, they accounted for about one-third of my business." One day "Go Fly a Kite" decided it didn't want to fly Marblehead Kites anymore so it informed Breuhaus it wasn't going to distribute her wares. In effect, she was told to go fly a kite.

Fortunately, Breuhaus was undaunted and now does 30-to-40 percent of her sales through sales reps who get between a 15-to-20 percent commission, usually 15 percent. The rest of the sales are done directly through Marblehead Kite. She was able to take up the slack by selling a little harder and a little more often on her own.

It's important not to rely solely on one outlet for sales that you don't have control over. If Natural Choice uses a manufacturer to distribute products, it won't be giving up the ship because it will still be doing the marketing in conjunction with the manufacturer; and it will still, in some cases, be using its own brokers. In the short run, by getting someone else to do the manufacturing *and* brokering, the company's attention can go more towards its marketing strength.

"Our thrust," explains Scaife, "is that if we can deal with an established manufacturer, it takes a tremendous burden off of us and lets us concentrate on what we're best at—advertising, promotions, and marketing. That's our goal."

MARKETING MESSAGES

It takes more than one outlet to make a market. Don't allow your business to be crippled by putting all the eggs in one nest. Find alternatives—brokers, manufacturers, distributors.

Throw out more than one idea and hope one sticks. If one stream of selling doesn't pan out, try another. Keep at it. Use all the methods you can think of to sell your product profitably without diminishing its value to the market.

Use a combination of strategies. Mix your plays and plans. This gives you a better chance to gain a strong market position against the competition.

Chapter Twenty-Five

Selling the Staff on Selling

It's an interesting feeling to finally reach the point of the book that most readers probably thought would be the thrust of the whole epic—selling. When I first discussed a book on marketing with some of my editors and friends outside of the business world, their immediate response was, "Marketing is selling. Selling is marketing. The two are the same, no?" No. But that point should be obvious to you by now, having journeyed through Grand Forks, Madison, Passaic, Hudson, and other outposts to learn just what it is that goes into marketing.

None of this is to say that selling is not a crucial aspect of marketing. It's like that old Rube Goldberg-type board game that was popular in the late 1960s or early 1970s called *Mousetrap.* Slowly you build an elaborate trap, adding piece-by-piece, until finally you get a beautifully synchronized dream of a machine that pounces a painless cage over a tiny little plastic mouse.

With marketing, all the pieces we've come across so far in the journey fit together to reach the goal of getting the product to the consumer, having the consumer pay, and turning a profit. The marketing amalgam might not be as rickety as that old mousetrap, but all the care, joy, and creativity that went into the mousetrap should go into your marketing.

Selling is crucial to the process. Dealing with the sales staff if there is one, even if it's one person, is crucial. Many entrepreneurs manage and compensate their sales staffs differently, and most of the techniques are startlingly old-fashioned in small to midsize businesses. Learn the market, compensate the people for their success in the marketplace, and don't automatically pay them so much that you might start killing their motivation.

Training the Sales Staff

Mary Sprague's sales staff had the sales technique down in her New York City Victory Shirt stores. But when they moved into shopping mall settings in Bethesda, Maryland, and Fairfax, Virginia, boy, were they in for a surprise.

"A different kind of people went to the mall than in New York. In D.C., the super-responsiveness that we gave in New York was intimidating to the customer. No one strolls on Madison Avenue. But in D.C., the consumer was terrified," says Mary.

So Victory changed its technique. Rather than use the service-only-may-I-help-you-right-away approach that had been so successful in the New York stores, Sprague shifted the emphasis to a much softer approach in the mall stores to make the customers feel more comfortable browsing.

"A different kind of people go to the malls than shop in New York. We became dependent on mall traffic. In New York, the customer wanted to be taken care of quickly—bin, ban, thank you man."

Not so in the D.C. area malls. Sprague trains her sales staff accordingly, depending on whether they'll be in the mall stores or in the New York City stores. "We can probably start a salesperson after two weeks of constant training. Not let them loose. That'll take six weeks if they're lucky. We want them to be able to handle the consumer's questions and concerns, and get a sale in a knowledgeable, intelligent way.

"We market ourselves as the 'shirt experts,' and we pride ourselves that our sales staff is knowledgeable."

Keeping the Sales Staff

Once you've got them trained, the trick is to keep them. And for some, that's a trick indeed. Generally turnover rates in sales staff depend on many factors, including working conditions, regional opportunities, and opportunities within the business. Stephen Garber, of London Wine Company, is in the center of a very competitive wine trade, so turnover can be somewhat frequent at his shop. "In retail, it's rather difficult to keep talented people," he says. "When they get to the top, they often find themselves in a box.

"You're lucky to have your top people more than two or three years, unless you can give them some logical avenue to grow into. But don't forget, this is still a small business. We're not General Motors here."

Most recently, Garber lost his former controller because she left to buy her own retail wine business. "She was that bright that she knew she could do it for herself," says Garber. "When you work with good people, this is what happens."

Those further from metropolitan areas don't always have the same turnover problems. Sometimes this results from the fact that it's not terribly difficult to make your place more attractive to work for than anybody else's place in town, simply because there aren't so many other places around.

Hal Gershman, of Happy Harry's Bottle Shop, has had several of the same key people work with him in his liquor store more than nine years. "We have a very low turnover of key people because we pay at the absolute upper end of scale for key people in North Dakota—straight salary with a good benefits plan.

"We don't punch clocks here. All five of my key people have three weeks paid vacation, but I don't keep a record of vacation time. They have a sense of freedom with their job that I like to feel with my work, too. My managers understand that at three o'clock on Mondays, Tuesdays, and Wednesdays, I go to take care of my daughter."

Settings in areas that are not feeder cities to larger metropolitan areas seem to boast lower rates of turnovers than those right in the pulsebeat of the competitive job market. The reasons for this are fairly obvious. With fewer companies in the smaller markets, there are fewer vertical shifts in jobs. If an employer makes life good and rewarding, there might be a greater tendency to stay.

Al Felly thinks so. In fact, his Felly's Flowers' downtown store manager has been there since Felly opened shop in 1949. His executive assistant, Eadie Graham, who's been with Felly's for 19 years, was the east side store manager for 13 years, where she established the highest productivity in the history of Felly's Flowers. "This is my family," Felly insists.

"We'd rather start people in our own stores than hire them away from other stores, because it takes us six months to break them of what they've learned at the other places," says Felly.

Compensating the Sales Staff

When it comes time to compensate the sales staff, David Gilvar doesn't care where they came from as long as they can sell the product. Gilvar is president of Outline, Inc., a manufacturer of lightweight, modular display systems. The hardware itself can run for around $2,500. But the sales pitch is a bit more tricky, because Gilvar's people also sell the graphics that go inside the frames. The whole unit, with graphics, can run about $4,000. For their success, Outline salespeople are rewarded quite nicely.

"Every salesperson can sell at least $300,000 worth of product a year," says Gilvar, slumping down in his office chair in Walpole. Gilvar, in light gray slacks, blue striped open-colored shirt, and blue blazer, is tall, tan, and slender, and could be a stand-in for actor James Caan. Some would probably think he could sell anything to anybody. And he probably has.

"We pay our people a 12.5 percent commission on gross sales. If they sell more than $60,000 worth of product in a quarter, they get an extra 5 percent on everything over the $60,000.

"One of our saleswomen in New York City did $250,000 in sales in the last quarter—in three months! That's $30,000 for sales and another $9,000 for her bonus. We had hired her as our first receptionist. Then she became our first bookkeeper. She sort of worked her way out of a job. We told her we'd guarantee her salary for six months if she'd just give selling a try."

Gilvar says "a lot" of his sellers have $100,000 sales months. "We think everyone should generate at least $25,000-a-month," says Gilvar, implying they won't be around long if they don't. "The average salesperson we have does enough to generate $300,000 in sales a year. Since we have around 60 trained salespeople, we figure there will be little problem growing to a total of $18 million in sales a year." In 1984, Outline's total sales were $9 million.

"We have a good reputation. The market's there," says Gilvar. But he doesn't want to blow the reputation or the potential market by using a salesforce that can't sell the product. He wants people with the drive and the finesse to sell a high-priced product.

MARKETING MESSAGES

Love thy sellers. Your salespeople form a smoothly synchronized marketing machine. Let them know their worth. Provide a good working atmosphere and plenty of salary incentives based on performance.

Motivate to win. Let your salespeople know that what they do and how they do it is important. Remember Maslow's point that productive people need to know what they're worth in tangible ways. Your reputation in the market and your bottom line depends on it.

Chapter Twenty-Six

The Pitch

It's a bright spring morning when I enter the Waltham, Massachusetts, showroom of Outline, Inc., to meet one of the company's top salesmen, Bob Abramson.

Outline's president, David Gilvar, has set up the meeting with complete confidence. Abramson is one of the first people Gilvar hired back in 1979, when Outline went on the market with its lightweight, modular display exhibit system. According to Gilvar, Abramson is a real "pitcher," which is something more than your usual salesman. Abramson is motivated, a problem-solver, the consummate professional.

Gilvar has set me up to Abramson as a prospective buyer, which really isn't far from the truth. After all, if Outline's product is so good, then even a writer like me should find good use for a display system. So I've come to be "pitched."

Bob Abramson is a tall man. That's the first thing that strikes me, because I have to look up at his face when I shake his hand. He's a dead-ringer for Jerry Orbach, the veteran Broadway actor, who played in the film *Prince of the City*. Abramson is distinguished-looking, graying, dressed in an impeccable light gray pin-stripe, and he's ready to sell.

It's clear he knows something of the set up. The gist of it, he thinks, is that he's supposed to sell me, but shouldn't expect me to buy anything, which is good because these units can go for several thousand dollars.

Abramson motions to a table and some chairs in the showroom and suggests we sit for a few minutes. The showroom is a large, very high ceilinged room; black ceiling, baby spot lights and track lighting all around. Various Outline displays are set up for good dramatic effect. There's a back-lighted skyline of Houston off to one side, and a cubicle-shaped Statue of Liberty display in one corner. The showroom may be enough in itself to close some deals. But then the buyer would miss Abramson's pitch.

Breaking the Ice

Abramson tells me he's been in sales for 30 years, that he started out as a press agent feeding material to columnists such as Bennett Cerf in the 1950s. His first real sales job was with Arrow Shirts in Chicago. Slowly he builds, gets a little information from me, gives me a little about himself, jokes about how when he was first selling the Outline displays all he had was a brochure written in Swedish. "If I didn't run into a Swede, I'd be in trouble," he laughs. When he senses the timing is right, he slides into the pitch.

"Let me see how maybe I can adapt this system to what you do for a living," he says as he steps around to the front of the table with his sample modular display unit. "You're not a typical prospect for Outline by any means. Are you? But I think it shows the versatility of our product."

Problem Solvers

Abramson is soothingly confident.

"I think the salesman of the past, the order-taker or the guy with the jokes, is a dying breed," Abramson confides. "The salesmen of the 1980s are the problem solvers. And to solve a problem you have to have a problem. If you ask enough questions, you get the problems out.

"We try in the beginning to find out something about the prospect. What the company's product or service is and any particular problems in marketing that product or service. Because of the versatility of our product we can quickly adapt it.

"In your particular case," Abramson says, having circled the camp and zeroed in on the target, "if you're writing a book there may be a couple of different situations where Outline can help you."

"At book fairs, which are notoriously bad in their exhibits, they have tables with books on them," Abramson says incredulously. "The object is to get the books out, of course. But wouldn't it be better if you had the cover of your book blown up eight-to-ten feet as a backdrop, instead of a curtain and pipes behind the books? It doesn't have to replace the books, but it can stop traffic. Because the number one problem that we see in trade shows or book fairs is the tendency to put too many photos and too much copy on an exhibit.

"The Tradeshow Exhibitors Association estimates that you've got 1.8 seconds to stop that body moving by your booth. With the confusion of the tradeshow, the competition, and the pace, if you don't slow or stop that person, you've lost that individual. You're not going to stop them by having copy they can't read from ten feet away. And since we are more and more going into a visual world with television anyway, why not have the guts to take one picture and blow it up over ten feet?

"Once the person stops, it's a lot easier to engage him in conversation and show your brochures at that time. It beats grabbing him as he's moving by and pulling him into the booth. That's the old time sell. Now here's where Outline shines. I mean we can talk about the fact that this is portable, versatile system, and that you can do this and you can do that with it. But the number one reason that Outline has gone from a $1 million company to a $10 million company is the graphics capabilities."

Listening to Abramson I keep telling myself I know I don't need one of these things; I knew it before I came in here. But the lighting, the displays, the presentation, all mesh together in such a way that I also keep thinking, "Hey, one of these things might be good to have. This guy's not kidding. You need one of these numbers."

Abramson senses my glassy eyed interest. He's in his stride. He continues.

"In addition to book fairs, you may be in a situation where you'd be autographing books. Wouldn't it be ideal to have one even at bookstores?" Now Abramson heads for the ego. "You can't move around custom-built displays that way, but you can put this in the back of your car, go to a bookstore that's promoting your book, stick it up behind you, and go to town."

Selling Product Benefits

The Outline system when fully opened, stands around seven feet high. You swing the panels one way and open them another in an arc, and, if you follow Abramson's lead, you say "Voila!"

He's opened the system up and confides, "You know, one of the reasons I got into sales is that I'm very clumsy by nature. I'm not kidding. I think my mother dropped me on my head at an early age and damaged that portion of my brain. I can't conceptualize mechanical things. It's that bad.

"The reason I bring that up is not to dwell on my problems, but because there are a lot of people in the world like me." Abramson has managed to say that even a big galumph can set up this display. And he never had to insult me to make his point. In fact, he cleverly poked fun at himself by way of example.

"This system stands 6′8″," Abramson says. "But you noticed how quickly I was able to put it up. The key to the design is the 360-degree hinges. The hinges let you put it up quickly and let you make it into a six-panel unit from an eight-panel unit." He plays with the configuration of the display system, showing me that the world is my oyster, my dreams of great displays can come true. "And we've got it in the aluminum and also in the black behind you there," he says.

"You can zig-zag the system," he explains. "You can make a column configuration. And, any material three-sixteenths of an inch thick will fit in these channels. Each panel has two channels."

Abramson goes through at least 20 different configurations that the unit can provide. He talks about hidden slide projectors, rear lighting, plexiglass, computer messages, but chiefly about the graphics capabilities that Outline offers. "From conception to production, to end product, Outline has a full in-house organization for visual merchandise."

Abramson has delivered his pitch. It has been almost hypnotic.

Persistence

When he sits back down at the table, Abramson talks about selling generally.

"The toughest part of this job," he says, "especially for a new man, is to get on that phone at 9 o'clock every morning and make 40 or 50 phone calls and wind up with 40 or 50 rejections. At the end of the day you might not have made one appointment.

"But if you're philosophical about it, the next day you might call up at 9 o'clock and the guy on the other end will say, 'Wow! We were just talking about something like that at a meeting a half hour ago! Are you a mind reader?' And when that happens, don't leave that phone because you start to get hot. I don't know how it works, but some days everybody you talk to is interested. When that happens, do not even stop to eat lunch."

Not every sales pitch is the same, of course. Outline has a fairly high-priced product and it often caters to a fairly sophisticated clientele. Abramson says it takes about 40 calls to make a single sale. Obviously, for someone selling a cheaper item, this would be unbearable. But when you figure the Outline product is selling for $4,000, graphics and all, that's not bad.

The Old-Fashioned Pitch

I remember when my sister visited me after I'd lived in Boston for about a year. She was living in the Midwest and working as a nutritionist for the Sioux Indians, so her encounters with sales pitches were something of an anomaly.

We were walking in the Downtown Crossing area of Boston, a pedestrian-only street. Here were the famous bargain basement Filene's, and dozens of other department, jewelry, book, and specialty stores. On one corner, outside of what has to be one of the largest Woolworth's, was a salesman wearing an apron and a microphone, and selling some kind of slices/dices carvings knives. It was bargain city. If you bought this, you got that; but if you did this now, you got something else—but only now did you get this if you did that.

The salesman pitched fast. It was like watching an old-time revival meeting. People were rushing up to him, making multiple purchases. He was curing them of their kitchen woes and giving them a free gift to boot. When I looked around, I realized my sister was no longer at my side. She had rushed to the front of the crowd and was purchasing enough knives to seat the entire Sioux Indian nation at a sit-down dinner. She had fallen for the pitch.

I thought about this as I arrived at Boston's Haymarket, where farmers sell fresh goods at rock-bottom prices from old wheelcarts. After a day with Outline's Bob Abramson, and having recalled the "slice 'um, dice 'um king" on the drive into Boston, I am primed for the Haymarket. The place is full of pure sales pitch. "Get your freshest tomatoes here," or "Eggplant, three for a dollar here." Everybody sells the same goods, but to the individual sellers it's all different and better than what the next fellow is selling.

And there's the butcher who's been standing at the door of Carl's Meat Market for years. His pitch is point-blank simplicity. As every passerby walks through the crowd, he leans forward and blurts out, "Want some meat?" Those who haven't been to the market don't know what to make of him. Some ignore him. Others chuckle a little, say, "Oh, okay," and go inside where one of the other butchers will wait on them, describing the nuances of trim, cut, weight. Out on the street the sales pitch continues like an ancient chant: "Want some meat? Want some meat?"

What a contrast to the approach taken by salesmen like Bob Abramson of Outline, Inc. Yet, in many ways, each message is designed for the specific needs of the market. It's to be expected that a sales pitch for a graphics display unit will differ from one designed to sell meat. If Abramson is sophisticated and subtle, the meat man is no less effective with his simple single-liner aimed at the gut.

I double park on Clinton street, get out, and walk to the Haymarket. I think I could use a good cut of meat today.

Marketing Messages

Solve a problem. Meet a need. The key to a successful sales pitch is that your customer has to want what you're selling. By presenting your product as a solution to a problem you can help the buyer recognize that need.

Every pitch is the first pitch. Be persistent, stay fresh. If you make 20 sales pitches with no results, accept it as part of the game. Keep at it. When you find a customer who needs your product or service, there are likely to be many more waiting in line.

Chapter Twenty-Seven

Give Me Some of That Old-Time Selling

So this is how it ends. On a cold, damp Friday night in Boonton, New Jersey. It's dark on Division Street. About the only light is the refection of the moon in thc paintwork of the cars parked bumper-to-bumper for about three-quarters of a mile up and down this street. There are no stores on this stretch of the street, no movie theaters, no restaurants, not even a shopping mall.

People have come here for the Old Feed Mill Auction. Every other Friday night at 7 o'clock they pack into the gallery room, once part of the Old Feed Mill Store in Boonton. In 1978, it was transformed into what has to be one of the most popular hits since George Burns and Gracie Allen played a one-night stand in a Boonton theater.

Jack Wootton's family started the feed mill business in 1892. The building now used for the auction has been around since 1904. When the feed mill business dried up in 1978, Jack decided to put the building to good use by running regular Old Feed Mill Auctions.

"My grandfather had told me you'd never starve to death in the feed business, because people will always need feed," Wootton says.

It's ironic that the auctions at the Old Feed Mill are the same sales mechanisms used to sell-off the assets of the many farms that have been suffering liquidations over the past couple of years. No one, not even Jack Wootton's grandfather, foresaw the economic plight the American farmer would go through in our time.

Jack Wootton is an elfin-looking sort of man. His regular dress is an Oxford cloth button down collar shirt and chino pants. He hefts quite a paunch and sports a Lincolnesque beard. As an auctioneer, Wootton specializes in collectible Americana, which is a broad category that includes anything from toys to jewels to some furnishings to "whorehouse tokens," once used to gain entry into local brothels. But Wootton is quick to point out that he won't auction off junk. "Auctions are generally thought of as whorehouses of garbage. With our sales, it's collectible or we don't sell it," Wootton insists.

He got into the auction business quite by accident. "I started in the auction business in Marathon, Florida, in 1971," Jack recalls. "I was vacationing in the Keys and was bored in Marathon. St. Colombo's Episcopal Church was having a flea market, so I wandered down. They were selling things to build an education wing on the church and they were doing poorly. I was sitting there seeing silver practically being given away. I went to the parish priest and told him I could do better. I started at 11 a.m. and went to 4 p.m. and raised $4,000 for the church. They called me up the next year and asked me back."

A "Certain Charm" to an Auction Sell

On the front of Jack Wootton's auctioneer's podium is a little brass plaque which reads, "The difference between men and boys is the price of their toys." Every other Friday night, his audiences of 400-plus cram into an area big enough for probably 250, registers, gets a paper plate with a number on it, and holds those paper plates up to prove the plaque correct.

While in the gallery area where the sales are held every other Friday night, Wootton talked about auctioning and how he got caught up in the business. While he's very affable, he's really a challenge to talk to. He'll tell you anything and everything and then some, but he rambles. And what's slightly more nerve racking is the fact that he paces when he talks.

"There's a certain charm to this Old Feed Mill thing," Wootton boasts. "In New Jersey, there are probably 150 auctioneers — it's up there in volume. But in what I specialize in, I'm probably the leader. In the prestige area of collectible Americana, we're it in new Jersey." Wootton figures in terms of sales, he probably ranks around sixth in total dollar volume of all auctioneers in New Jersey.

"We command some respect in New Jersey," says Wootton. "In New Jersey, we're it."

The Cost of Getting Known

Although the place is packed on auction nights these days, and almost all of the commissions he makes are pure profit since he owns the building, the first years of the Old Feed Mill Auctions were a bit rough.

"The first two years for the gallery—1978 and 1979— were both losers," Wootton confides. "It was the cost of getting known. It's tough to establish yourself.

While he's not talking specifics, his profits in 1983 and 1984 certainly hovered in the "substantial" range, and more than made up for his initial losses. "This is generally a profitable business," Wootton says as he paces the creaky floor. "The truth of the matter is that the auction business is *very* profitable."

While Wootton might do a limited mailing to people who registered at his previous auctions—which, to bid, you must do— most of the crowd comes from word of mouth. Wootton gets a lot of repeat business. When he mails 300 announcements to previous attendees, he says at least half will come. He also runs a recorded message the week leading up to the auction to give people an idea what's going to be featured.

How the Auction Works

Since Wootton works full-time at another job, people who want to auction their collectibles must bring them in to the gallery the Sunday prior to a Friday night auction. At that time it's registered and readied in the gallery. "People come from the Metropolitan New York area, but also from Delaware and Maryland. The fact that it's Boonton doesn't mean that it's only a Boonton audience," he says.

Wootton takes between a 10-and-25 percent commission on sales, depending on his arrangement with the seller. "We probably have about $15,000 worth of stuff here," he says, gesturing around the gallery room. "The average sale is $35,000-to-$40,000. The current offerings are such a hodgepodge. When you have an estate or a liquidation, this place will be filled to the rafters with stuff.

"We sell all the stuff off on auction night," he says. He ponders, assessing how much these current items will bring in. "Fifteen thousand, yes. It'll be $15,000 almost exactly. I'm not very far off very often."

Building Confidence in the Auctioneer

Wootton also admits some of his bad habits as an auctioneer. One is "instant appraising," the other letting the customers know when they're being ridiculous about a bid.

"I have a bad habit of appraising something in front of the crowd when I say, 'How about $500?' and then drop the bidding down and get it back up to $500 anyway," Wootton says. "I do almost an instant appraisal.

"I also almost always stop it when the people overbid. You have to have confidence in the auctioneer. Stopping people from spending too much is real good. I'll stop the auction, rap the gavel, and say, 'You're not listening.' This gives me real credibility. There are so many good things around. Chicanery and nonsense don't bring back a lot of return."

Wootton walks around the gallery, giving little previews of what the buyers will bid on. There's an old comic book called "This Is Communism," which Wootton says lists for $150. And there are also some actual "whorehouse tokens" from a collector out in Randolph Township.

He walks over to an oak china cabinet, which Wootton says is a Larkin brand. "The name is magic. When people hear the name, it sells. It was popular in the Sears catalog from 1895 to 1910. It'll probably bring around $1,000 tonight. New, it cost almost $25. It's the best thing in the sale tonight. There's also this early pine cupboard from around 1810 or 1820. It'll go for around $300. This art deco table from 1925 is broken—one of the wings is missing. But it'll probably go for $25. This primitive jam cupboard may be a sleeper, but it'll bring $125 to $150."

The night of the auction I find a parking spot in front of the old Boonton Molding Plant, and walk a quarter of mile down Division Street to the Old Feed Mill. It's a cold night. The auction has already begun. You can hear the crowd murmur from a distance. "Terry's Chuck Wagon" is parked outside the gallery doors, selling hot and cold drinks, burgers, and other comestibles to hungry auction goers.

The place is packed. it's hard to figure out how all these people jammed themselves in here. And this, Wootton said earlier, wasn't even going to be a big night. Some people sit in folding chairs; some stand. Others, if they could, would pace.

From the doorway to the gallery you can hear Jack Wootton clearly as he does his auctioning. It's like listening to a Hebrew cantor at high holiday services. He melodiously chants out the bidding wars as they're going on, urging a price hike by lifting his chant a tone, and then singing out the final price at the end, with a bang of the gavel.

I register and wait for my paper plate and number. I know I'm going to buy something tonight. Preferably something warm.

"Three-hundred-and-fifty-dollars-sold," Wootton sings out as he bangs the gavel. George and Gracie would have loved it.

MARKETING MESSAGES

Create a special buying ambience. The lesson of the auction sell is its charm. Buyers feel good about what they're buying and where they're buying it. This makes for confidence that keeps them coming back for more.

There's magic in the old-time sell. This means an honest, down-to-earth salesman. Marketing this homey nice-to-see-you-again atmosphere pays off for buyer and seller alike.

Index

About The Author

Jeffrey L. Seglin is a writer and editor whose articles have appeared in *Inc.*, *Venture*, *Boston*, *Financial Planning*, *TV Guide*, *Goodlife*, *Banker & Tradesman*, *Personal Investing*, *Enter*, and other publications. He is a contributing editor to *Financial Planning* and *Goodlife* magazines, as well as the personal finance writer for *Boston* magazine.

He was the content editor for Public Broadcasting System's "On The Money" national television series and serves as a consulting editor to Random House's Professional Publishing Group. Seglin is also the author of several business books.

He has worked on marketing projects for Digital Computer Corporation, The Children's Hospital, and a host of other organizations. He lives in Boston, Massachusetts.